British Design since 1880

Fiona MacCarthy

British Design since 1880

A Visual History

Lund Humphries · London

First edition 1982
Published by
Lund Humphries Publishers Ltd
26 Litchfield Street London WC2

SBN 85331 447 0 (paperback)
SBN 85331 461 6 (casebound)

Designed by Herbert and Mafalda Spencer
Printed in Great Britain by Jolly & Barber Ltd, Rugby

Photographic acknowledgements:

BBC   105

David Carter Associates   219

Dinah Casson   206

Christie's   33

Clareville Studios Ltd   26, 149, 151, 153, 155, 182, 185, 192, 193, 208, 211

Keith Collie   218

Conran Associates   28, 179

Lucienne Day   165

Design Council   156, 161–4, 166–9, 172, 174, 177, 178, 184, 186, 191, 194–9, 216, 220, 221, 226

Mark Fiennes   214

Kenneth Grange   227

Heal & Son Ltd   106

David Higham   3, 5, 6, 11–14, 17–24

London Transport Executive   125, 127

John Maltby   201

Mann Studios   147, 183

Gordon McLeish   1, 2, 7, 8, 9, 10, 15, 16, 27, 41–6, 49, 53–8, 64, 67, 68, 70–8, 82–5, 87–9, 94, 96, 98, 103, 108–13, 119, 120, 121, 122–4, 128–35, 137, 140, 141, 142, 145, 152, 157, 160, 170, 171, 173, 202, 207, 212, 213, 215

William Morris Gallery, Walthamstow   4

Ogle Design   223

Plush-Kicker   176

Race Furniture   144

John Rose & John Dyble   146

Gordon Russell Ltd   148

Leiga Siegelmann   203

Sotheby's Belgravia   102

Victoria & Albert Museum   38, 40, 99, 204

Josiah Wedgwood & Sons Ltd   136, 138, 158, 159

Robert Welch   187

Contents

Preface

For a century or more, from William Morris onwards, there has been an easily identifiable strain in society in Britain concerned with the improvement of the objects which we use and live with. This movement for reform has, through the years, developed certain ideas on the designer's social role as well as recognisable criteria on aesthetics. From the Arts and Crafts movement of the late nineteenth century, the Design and Industries Association campaigns between the wars, through to the post-war Council of Industrial Design (now the Design Council), a tradition has evolved which is, I would claim, particularly British: a tradition in the approach to designing and a tradition in reaching the solutions, amounting to a long succession of products, both handmade and mass-produced, with a common visual character. Indeed, the idea that consistent standards are both practically possible and morally desirable, that design solutions can be measured against a sense of ideal rightness, both functional and aesthetic, has dominated much of British design thinking over the past century. It is a concept in which, from the 1930s onwards, the British government has been investing ever-increasing resources, especially in the education of designers, and since the war it has been at the very centre of activities in government-approved design.

The design movement of the past hundred years has created its own *species humaniores*, the genus which in the early days was known as 'art adviser' but which we are more likely now to designate 'designer'. The designer's professional status has become increasingly sophisticated, but the basic role remains that of problem solver, reconciler of conflicting demands and outside pressures. When it comes down to it, it is the designer who makes the creative leap, the visual synthesis. Designers finally decide how things shall *be*.

The degree of pure creativity, the freedom allowed to the designer in arriving at the object, of course is variable. With a one-off piece of pottery, handmade in a craft workshop, extra-aesthetic pressures are relatively minimal: attention must be paid to techniques and to materials and (possibly) to function and (possibly) to marketing; but the art-content is the factor which is dominant. Moving on to, for instance, a chair for mass production there are wider considerations, far beyond the basic requirements of techniques and materials: functioning and marketing acquire much more importance; there are the added pressures of company image and corporate investment. In this kind of context, the aesthetic contribution is one of many elements, though still a major one. By the time one reaches the designer's contribution to, say, a machine tool or microprocessor, the purely aesthetic aspects are in effect subsidiary; the designer's role is a collaborative one, working in conjunction with the engineer, providing a relatively small, though still essential, element of visual and functional coherence from within a whole network of alternative criteria. And yet, in the end, is the process very different? Though different in degree, in the extent of its restraints, the process of arriving at the ultimate decision is, I would argue, much the same in kind whether one is designing a piece of handmade silver or acting as design consultant for the High-Speed Train. It is still a question of aesthetic judgment, the designer is still making the creative leap, the synthesis, and it is the broad base of this reconciling talent, the designer's special role in each successive period in bringing the various conflicting design factors to the optimum visual and functional solution, which is one of the basic tenets of this book.

The idea for the book came from an exhibition – 'Homespun to Highspeed: A Century of British Design 1880–1980' – which I organised in 1979 for Sheffield City Art Galleries. This was not so much a collection of the objects I most like (though personal predilections do, of course, come into it), as an attempt to collect together what I saw as the key pieces in the British design movement, by which I mean the élite, progressive movement, over the past century. I wanted to assemble the designs which seemed important in their day, objects then approved of by the cognoscenti, as well as things which still seem very good solutions to their particular set of design pressures, expressions of the vitality and excellence of their particular period of design. By collecting together many hundreds of examples of designers' work over this long period, I hoped to discover – and indeed to reveal – some salient facts about designers, their aims and aspirations, what they felt they were about. This visual record, based on the selection of exhibits, attempts a distillation of what is, to me anyway, an infinitely interesting aspect of recent British culture. I hope others think so too.

I feel it is important to mention in passing the continuing, perhaps even increasing, elusiveness of actual examples of British design of the immediate past period. This seems strange when one considers contemporary concern for the national artistic heritage in general, and the recent growth of interest in design history at both amateur and academic levels. But the cavalier attitude towards major design-historic acquisitions, chaotically organised and erratically catalogued even in some areas of our best-known national collections, is surely a cause for some concern. Admittedly this gave my own research a certain piquancy, a sense of the excitement which must be quite familiar to archaeologists at work on a new site, as, for instance, past Design Centre Awards were excavated from the cellars of South Kensington and a massive hoard of 1930s glass and ceramics, still packed in the tea-chests in which it was delivered, was uncovered in the store-rooms of one of the most famous of provincial city art galleries. There are, of course, exceptions: the superbly well-kept and immaculately documented collection of textiles at the Whitworth Art Gallery in Manchester; the displays of furniture by Gimson and the Barnsleys at Leicester and at Cheltenham, crucial national collections which still retain a very individual quality, reflecting the enthusiasms of their keepers; the beautiful, small-scale Bath Crafts Study Centre; the logically organised, professionally catalogued modern silver collection at Goldsmiths' Hall in London.

These collections are all models of their kind. There are also some signs of an increasing sense of responsibility towards their own past products by such manufacturers as Warner and Sons Ltd, continuously building up a comprehensive archive, and Gordon Russell Ltd whose small design museum at their factory in Broadway is so personal and evocative it almost undermines institutionalised collecting. But these examples are very isolated. The fact is that many historic designs, including some which I had hoped to show in this recent exhibition, are already disappearing. This is especially true of products of the 1920s period and those of the 1940s and 1950s. These post-war designs in a sense appear so recent that their potential importance is neglected. There is much to be located before it is too late.

At the end of the book I have made a brief location list, based upon my travels, an outline indication of the major collections up and down the country. They are terribly far-flung. For the basic problem, which still seems no nearer a solution, is the all too obvious lack of a central British modern design collection where the main developments can be viewed in context as part of a whole historic sequence. So far, the collections all tend to be fragmented. The Crafts Council collection, though excellent, is totally craft-orientated. The Conran Foundation's Boilerhouse project, though again a highly welcome enterprise, is concentrated on industrial design. Apart from the Victoria and Albert Museum, where the British modern collections are richly comprehensive but displayed in such a random way as to be daunting to anyone except the most intrepid historians, there is nowhere in the country where one can follow through the pattern of modern design in all its aspects, the interaction of hand and machine production which has been so formative to the development of British design over the past century, in many ways the source of its great individuality and strength.

Fiona MacCarthy
November 1981

Acknowledgements

As well as the many owners of the objects illustrated, whose generosity is acknowledged in the picture list, I should like to thank Frank Constantine, Julian Spalding and James Hamilton, and other staff of Sheffield City Art Galleries, organisers of the 'Homespun to Highspeed' exhibition, without whom this book would never have materialised. Their enthusiasm has been very much appreciated.

I should also like to express our gratitude for the considerable and very expert contribution made by Gordon McLeish to the photographic content of this book. This is detailed in the photographic credits on page 4.

My view of British design has built up slowly, over many years, and I am very grateful to the dozens, if not hundreds, of people who have endlessly – and usually enjoyably – discussed the subject with me. Indeed, this applies to almost everyone I know.

For special information relating to this book I need to thank the following: Nick Butler, Frank Height, Tom Karen, Bridget Kinally, Rodney Kinsman, Mary Mullin, James Pilditch, Robert Strand.

The British Tradition in Design

If anybody asked me to make up a short-list of the ten most British designs of the past century, this would be it:

One of Christopher Dresser's startlingly innovative metalwork designs of c.1880: British design at its most brilliant and precise.

A William Morris chintz.

A Gimson ladderback chair in ash, epitome of the ruralist traditional, homely yet very subtle, dominating British design till 1930.

A pre-war Murphy radio cabinet, designed by R.D.Russell.

Maybe (and this is, I suppose, an outside entry, but surely defensible as a prime example of the affectionate and quirky tendencies in the character of British design), one of the decorative pottery designs which Eric Ravilious did for Wedgwood in the 1930s.

A Race chair, as seen at the Festival of Britain, 1951.

A lighting design by Robert Heritage for Rotaflex, an admirable example of the reappearance of old Design and Industries Association principles of common-sense and rightness in product designing in the post-war period.

A Shirley Craven fabric, superb illustration of mid-1960s jollity and style.

A spectacular piece of Craft Revival furniture of the 1970s, when the decorative individualistic urges, surprisingly, resurfaced.

A High-Speed Train.

All these, I would maintain, have a common basis in a particular, peculiarly British tradition of designing, and most are illustrated later in the book.

What this tradition is, what ideas most inspired it, are the things I shall be analysing in this introduction. They were important ideas which had their origins in the Arts and Crafts movement of the late nineteenth century and which can be followed right through to present-day British design practice. In attempting to explain them, I can do no better than to start quite near the middle, with the words of Frank Pick, the famous Chief Executive of the London Transport Passenger Board in the period between the two World Wars, Chairman of the DIA, Chairman of the Council for Art and Industry (precursor of the Design Council) in the 1930s, for whom design was almost a religion. Speaking to the DIA in Edinburgh he said:

11

'Everything is made for a use. The test of the goodness of a thing is its fitness for that use. So that boots eked out with canvas or paper, or fashioned of porous leather, are no good, for the essence of a boot is to keep the foot dry. So that flower-vases with narrow bottoms that topple over and make a mess are no good. So that a salt-pot in metal that corrodes with the natural dampness of the salt is no good. So that posters ornamented and confused until the words cannot be read at a glance (the main requirements of a poster) are no good. If you will keep an alert mind you can multiply examples from the common objects you meet with everyday. The test of the goodness of a thing is its fitness for use. If it fails on this first test, no amount of ornamentation or finish will make it any better; it will only make it more expensive, more foolish.'[1]

So much of what he says is central to the thinking of the British design movement. The functional aesthetic: the relation of practicality to beauty. The preoccupation with small things of daily life: the flower-vases, salt-pots and the boots which keep the rain out. (Boots were also an obsession with W.R.Lethaby.) The common-sense approach, homely yet highminded; the emphasis on plainness; the rejection of extravagance, dismissal of the foolish. The tone of voice so kindly and so certain. Solid stuff.

Good design is really a statement of the obvious. This perception of a fact which has proved not altogether as plain as one might think has been one of the main principles of the design reformers. It helps illuminate the good sense and moderation in British design in the past century. The insistence on fitness for use as a means to and a correlation of beauty can quite well be traced back from Frank Pick to William Morris. Like Pick, William Morris was concerned with humble detail, with making the daily round more orderly and seemly, as part of his whole urge to reorganise society, his large hopes for getting rid of the superfluous and pompous. Ideals of simple usefulness of course abounded in the Arts and Crafts movement and they find their best expression in the speeches and writings of W.R.Lethaby, disciple of Morris and a master of the aphorism. (He once said: 'Gothic cathedrals are as natural as birds' nests'.) Lethaby had some strong views on the role of the designer, maintaining that the best design was basic, never showy. Here he is at his most forthright, in some lines from *Art and Workmanship*:

'Art is not a special sauce applied to ordinary cooking; it is the cooking itself if it is good. Most simply and generally art may be thought of as *the well-doing of what needs doing*. If the thing is not worth doing it can hardly be a work of art, however well it may be done. A thing worth doing which is ill done is hardly a thing at all.'[2]

It was Lethaby's view that a machine-made product should be designed in such a way as to show quite obviously that it is the child of the machine; it is, he explains, the pretence and subterfuge of most machine-made things which make them so disgusting. A sense of the importance of honest sense of purpose, of calling a chair a chair, a boot a boot, together with distaste for the false and the effusive, characterises both the work and the pronouncements of the design reform groups of those early days.

One can also follow this same feeling going forward in British design history from Pick to Gordon Russell in his influential post as Director of the Council of

1
'Peacock' dish by William De Morgan, late 19th century, painted in fashionable Persian colours. Typically rich and fanciful De Morgan treatment of the Peacock motif, so powerful a symbol of the Aesthetic Movement. Victoria and Albert Museum.

2
Aesthetic pots with greeny-ochre glazes made by Linthorpe Art Pottery, c.1880, probably designed by Christopher Dresser, Art Designer to the pottery from its foundation in 1879. Handled flask from Stoke-on-Trent City Museum and Art Gallery; little jar from the collection of Mr and Mrs H.Ovenall.

3
'Medway' or 'Garden Tulip' block-printed chintz,
designed by William Morris, 1885, and printed at
Merton Abbey. An example of the nearness-to-nature
theme which obsessed Morris. He used the same design
to make a wallpaper. Whitworth Art Gallery, University
of Manchester.

4
'Wey' block-printed chintz, designed by William Morris,
1884. The name is taken from one of the tributaries of
the River Thames beside which Morris lived (both in
Oxfordshire and London): this is one of his many
river patterns of the period. William Morris Gallery,
Walthamstow.

5
'Tulip and Bird' reversible double-cloth, wool and silk, designed by C.F.A. Voysey, manufactured by Alexander Morton & Co., c.1896. One of the most beautiful of Voysey's long series of formalised bird-and-plant patterns. Whitworth Art Gallery, University of Manchester.

6
Embroidered table runner by May Morris, late 19th century. William Morris's younger daughter May took charge of the embroidery workshops of the Morris firm in 1885, when she was 23. Her patterns tend to be more static than her father's, more heraldic. William Morris Gallery, Walthamstow.

7
Bowl with flambé glaze by Bernard Moore, 1908.
Bernard Moore, working in North Staffordshire,
produced a succession of experimental glazes –
comparable with Pilkington's and Ruskin at that same
period – of an intense richness and great decorative
effect. Leicestershire Museums.

8
Large hand-painted porcelain 'Bird and Harebell' bowl
designed in 1908 by Hugh Thackeray Turner, Arts and
Crafts architect and designer, and Morris's successor as
secretary of the Society for the Protection of Ancient
Buildings. Victoria and Albert Museum.

9
Pottery with floral decoration, c.1920. The basic
Wedgwood shapes were hand-painted by Grace
Barnsley, daughter of Sidney Barnsley; the freshness and
delicacy of design is still very close to the Arts and Crafts
in feeling. From Mr and Mrs A.C.Davies's loan
collection in Leicestershire Museums.

10
Large dish with spotted deer, characteristic of the
widespread interest in *l'art sauvage* in the early 1920s,
designed by Truda Carter, hand-painted at Poole Pottery
and exhibited at the British Empire Exhibition in
Wembley in 1925. Museum Collection, Poole Pottery.

11
'Diagonal' cotton furnishing fabric by Phyllis Barron and Dorothy Larcher, one of many most original and confident designs for hand-block printed textiles, the work of a remarkably productive partnership of the 1920s and 1930s. Crafts Study Centre, Bath.

12
'Howarth' furnishing fabric in cotton and worsted/fibro designed by Marianne Straub for Helios, 1939. This particular shade of rusty-brown, so popular among the designers of that period, makes a final appearance among the Utility textiles of World War II, before giving way to the more acid-orange tones of the Festival of Britain. Marianne Straub.

13
'Wessex' hand-tufted wool rug from Wilton Royal
Carpet Manufacturing Co., c.1935; a swirling abstract
pattern unmistakably by Marion Dorn, mistress of the
modernist rug. Mrs J.Pruskin

14
Hand-tufted wool rug by John Tandy, c.1937, one of a
sequence of artist- and architect-designed rugs – by
McKnight Kauffer, Ronald Grierson, Marion Dorn,
Marian Pepler etc. – commissioned for limited production
by the Wilton Royal Carpet Manufacturing Co. from
1930 onwards. Note designer's signature in the bottom
corner, a very 1930s touch. Mrs J.Pruskin.

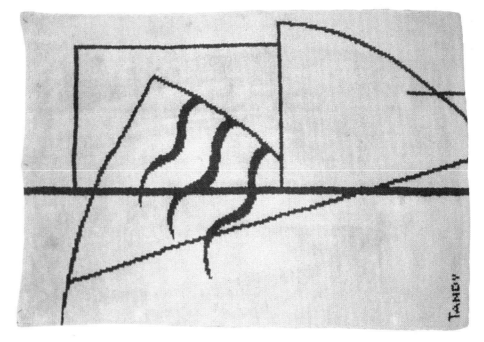

15
'Garden Implements' jug and lemonade beaker, designed
by Eric Ravilious for Wedgwood, 1937–8. This
decorative pattern, on standard Wedgwood Queen's
Ware shapes, was printed in sepia, with lustre decoration.
If Keith Murray's designs for Wedgwood in the 1930s
show the architect's approach to pottery, then this shows
the painter's: Ravilious at his most subtle and evocative.
Wedgwood Museum collection.

Industrial Design, from 1947 onwards. Gordon Russell's design philosophy was deeply practical, and British design, as approved by the Council of Industrial Design in the fifteen years which followed World War II, was indubitably honest and restrained and understated. It had to measure up to the Gordon Russell concept of 'the decent job', by which he meant a useful thing made well in the most suitable materials. The qualities of design admired by Gordon Russell were reflected in the choice for the Design Centre Awards given by the COID from 1957. The adjectives of praise bestowed on the first award winners range from 'practical', 'well-organised', 'agreeable' and 'pleasing' to 'plain but handsome', 'fresh and gay'. As Frank Pick had been much earlier, the judges of the 1950s were impressed by functional effectiveness and basic practicality, denoting a cast-iron room heater as 'an efficient appliance with a clean appearance which will fit appropriately into most surroundings', describing a range of pendant lampshades as 'light, durable and easily cleaned with soap and water' and praising the fitness for purpose of a new design in Melmex plastics tableware: 'The Judges were favourably impressed with the positive location of the cups in their saucers'. Good design was indeed, back in 1957, the statement of the obvious. But it was evidently something else as well. There is a definite sense of moral earnestness in the good design pronouncements of the day. Again, this is a tendency going back to Pick and Lethaby. Again, one reads it clearly in the comments of the judges of those first Design Awards: a set of cutlery, for instance, is praised highly for 'an elegance of style and an individuality of character which could only have developed from the careful consideration of the essential form of each article, coupled with a knowledge of the best of the past and a disciplined avoidance of those self-conscious departures from tradition characteristic of many contemporary designs'. This is surely a quintessentially British judgment on aesthetics, not just in its stress on elegance and unostentatious individuality (both favourite criteria of that early post-war period) but also in its ideas of humility and rightness, the belief that designers are not there to make a statement. A concept of good manners, of what is and is not done, a code which was soon challenged by the brashness of the 1960s, gives 1950s design its rather poignant sense of certainty, its comforting conviction of the lasting social value of the decent job well done.

The strongly moral bias of high design in Britain has its origins in the mid-Victorian reforming movements, in particular John Ruskin's passionate outcry against the prevailing conditions of work and standards of workmanship in an increasingly industrialised environment. His optimistic vision of the inherent beauty and potential creativity within society, only waiting to be rediscovered and released, was a powerful inspiration to the designers and design theorists of the Arts and Crafts movement. Ruskin saw the best design as a civilising instrument, a force for the good both of the man who makes the object and the society which ultimately uses it, and he puts forward a prophetic view of the importance of the designer's analytic way of working, a calm and measured, very systematic method, the basis of which is a true perception of human joy and humanitarian usefulness. Ruskin wrote:

'Without observation and experience, no design; without peace and pleasurableness in occupation, no design; and all the lecturings, and teachings,

and prizes, and principles of art in the world are of no use as long as you don't surround your men with happy influences and beautiful things.'[3]
In the writings of Ruskin one first finds this most beguiling idea of the designer as a benign influence within society, the solver of problems, smoother out of difficulties: the person whose large job it is to look at things afresh.

The long connection, from the Ruskin period onwards, with the radical political movements of the time gave British design a lasting sense of moral force and social purpose. The Arts and Crafts provided furniture for the New Life. There were strong links between many of the Arts and Crafts architects and designers and contemporary groups aligned to upturn the old order; these covered the whole spectrum of free-thinkers, from political and educational reformers to the people dedicated to new diet and new dress. Morris himself, of course, was politically active, increasingly so as he grew older, and his idealism, his view of the designer as reformer, as a kind of social catalyst, was transmitted to many Arts and Crafts designers. (I have always thought it particularly apt that the furniture designer Ernest Gimson, as a very young man, was first introduced to Morris after a meeting of the Leicester Secular Society: it was just that sort of world.) Morris's attitudes to the business of designing were shaped by his whole hatred of capitalist principles; as explained by J.W.Mackail, his first biographer: 'He carried on his business as a manufacturer not because he wished to make money, but because he wished to make the things he manufactured.' This purist view of the role of the designer, the rejection of the profit motive for the sake of impulses of social benevolence, a principle which has had so great an influence, for better or for worse, on British design development, comes pounding through in Morris's many speeches on art and life and their ideal interrelation, in none of them more strongly than his famous address on 'The Beauty of Life', given in Birmingham in 1880, in which he looks forward to 'the victorious days when millions of those who now sit in darkness will be enlightened by an *art made by the people and for the people, a joy to the maker and the user*'. He describes himself, and colleagues, as the servants of a cause.

Servants of a cause; bearers of the light; marchers with the banner; strikers of the colours: the British design movement over the past century has frequently been delineated in terms of battle and, rather intriguingly in view of the stalwart agnosticism of many of its leaders, has often been described in the images of muscular Christianity. It has been seen, simplistically, as a crusade: the powers of goodness ranged against commercial darkness. It has upheld principles of usefulness and beauty, appropriateness, simplicity and practicality as the proper birthright of the British people. From the early days of the Arts and Crafts it was, in theory at least, a very democratic movement. As Lethaby once put it: 'beauty can only be brought back to common life by our doing common work in an interesting way', and it was this democratic impulse which encouraged the cult of simplicity in Arts and Crafts aesthetics and inspired the late nineteenth-century peasant arts revival. The principle of common social responsibility, 'work of each for weal of all', was strikingly embodied in the Arts and Crafts guilds, the largest and best known of which, the Guild of Handicraft formed in 1888 by C.R.Ashbee, was conceived as an experiment in democratic practice. It was founded with an almost overwhelming sense of mission. Ashbee, over-ambitiously as it turned out, saw the Guild as the first phase of the regeneration of the nation, a revival which would spring from a new standard of beauty, new ideals of democratic work and life.

Though it never again reached such passionate expression, the idea that high standards of design are of importance to civilised life, the conviction – to put it at its baldest – that good design is a good thing, persisted. It is there in the campaigns of the DIA, from its foundation in 1915 onwards: the propaganda is replete with zeal and fervour; the members are undoubtedly still servants of the cause. One finds it just as strongly in the avant-garde design world of the 1930s, when the network of modern designers, manufacturers and shopkeepers tended to refer to themselves as 'real believers' and Alastair Morton of Edinburgh Weavers pointed out, at a DIA meeting, 'we cannot expect well-designed fabrics in an unstable or badly-designed society'. The designer's creative integrity was seen as a bulwark against commercial exploitation, the antithesis of Americanised 'styling' which so much shocked the British design pundits of the 1930s. The traditional British purity of purpose, the belief in design as a force for social betterment, gathered conviction in the years immediately after World War II, the heady period of 'Britain Can Make It' and the Festival of Britain, when the Council of Industrial Design saw itself empowered with the almost sacred charge of improving standards for the great mass of British people. Good design was seen to have a serious social purpose; the best design was clean and plain, not wayward or eccentric. The aim was to achieve a style accessible to everyone, a democratic style which was never ostentatious, not consciously 'designed' but real, simple and direct.

Although in recent years these principles have been much sabotaged, first by the jokers and then the profiteers, the altruistic elements within design in Britain have never been obliterated altogether. Even in the cynical and disillusioned 1970s, Professor Misha Black could still argue with conviction that it was the duty of designers to make certain that every system or object they initiated should celebrate the dignity of man. In an important article 'Fitness for what Purpose?' he argued that a humble, highly disciplined approach became, in a time of stringency, more, not less, essential; designers should renounce any formal preconceptions:

'We should approach each new problem from the base of practicality – how can it most economically be made, how will it function most effectively, how can maintenance be simplified, how can the use of scarce materials be minimised? An absolute concern with practicalities will produce new formal solutions as technology constantly develops: when alternatives present themselves during the design process, the aesthetic sensitivity of the designer will determine his selective decision but this should remain a searching process and not be seen as the opportunity for imposing a preconception of formal appropriateness. The difference between an arrogant conscious aesthetic and a conscientious searching for the most elegant solution is fundamental to my argument.'[4]

He wrote this in 1975. Not long ago.

British design has always been pervaded by a consciousness of what is the most natural solution to any given problem. This again goes back to Ruskin and his theories of the creative strength to be derived from the natural phenomena around us, and Morris's obsession with the English rural scene and with country traditions of sturdiness and honesty. The Arts and Crafts movement developed a romantic and indeed a highly sophisticated way of looking at the country life of England. The nearness to nature, to the rhythms of the seasons, the cycle of the harvest: the basic facts of rural life were almost glorified. There was a feeling that rural life was real life and that rural values, handed down the generations, were the truest and the purest. Rural quietness and slowness, the lack of incident, which was, to many country people, a privation, was to most of the Arts and Crafts architect-designers a source of inspiration. Their intense appreciation of the details of the English rural landscape – English villages and churches, English cottages and manors, the vernacular tradition in design and decoration, the use of country motifs, English flowers in English meadows – was important in its day and productive in its influence. From the Arts and Crafts emphasis on soundness and straightforwardness, the dignified and natural, there developed a whole attitude, belief in lasting values, which, one way or another, has been a constant element in British design practice.

The ruralist factor in design in Britain has often been bound up with the ideals of the simple life, the recurring conviction that civilisation has become so over-complex that the time has now come to sweep away the old accretions. To many supporters of the movement this implied not only simplified relationships, the breaking-down of age-old social barriers, but also simplified conditions of living, most ideally in a cottage in the country, with minimum possessions. Morris, Marshall, Faulkner & Co., Fine Art Workmen, founded in 1861 with the intention of protesting against prevailing styles of decoration, attempted a simplification by recreating a basic mediaevalism; Walter Crane described their aims as 'a revival of the mediaeval spirit (though not the letter) in design; a return to rich and suggestive surface decoration, and simple constructive forms'. Edward Carpenter, most famous of the British simple lifers, lived in a state of exemplary plainness in his cottage at Millthorpe in Derbyshire, from which he ruthlessly cleared out all unnecessary objects: 'the absence of THINGS' was noted with approval by Janet Ashbee, C.R.Ashbee's wife, who went to visit him. The impulse towards the free, untrammelled life was strong at the turn of the century, a period amazing for its variety of social experiment: 'At the bottom of my mind', wrote Lethaby, 'I long for the experience of standing up free and possessionless'. (This *cri de cœur* was heard again in the mid-1930s as visions of the minimum cottage were supplanted by the counter-attractions of minimum flats.)

For many early members of the Arts and Crafts societies, the love of rural life was mainly theoretical. But as the back-to-the-land movement gathered force, at the end of the nineteenth century, the exodus began: Gimson and the Barnsleys, and then Ashbee, to the Cotswolds; Godfrey Blount to Haslemere; and later Eric Gill to Ditchling. These, and other, rural communities of craftworkers, subscribing – more or less – to the old Ruskinian theory that lovely works of art can only be arrived at in a setting of corresponding truth and beauty, had enormous influence on the British design ethos. In particular, the furniture of Gimson and the Barnsleys, and the rural idioms which they adopted, the ruralist regard for sturdy, unpretentious structure, the countryman's tricks of champfering and chipcarving, contributed greatly to the sane and forthright character of twentieth-century design in Britain, creating the cult of the profoundly ordinary which has since then almost become the national style. Gordon Russell, as a young man working in the Cotswolds, was indubitably influenced by Gimson's furniture and by Gimson's whole approach to the design and making of it: his overall control of the details of the product through his own deep knowledge of materials and techniques.

In British design one finds great qualities of patience, the kind of doggedness one has to have to be a craftsman. The early DIA in fact exemplifies this outlook. Though their mission was improvement of design in British industry, several of the founders had their roots in rural craftsmanship. One thinks of Harry Peach, proprietor of Dryad handicrafts, earnest in his check tweed cap, his pockets stuffed with design pamphlets, embodiment of DIA right-thinking. Or Harold Stabler, as his colleague Hamilton Temple Smith described him: a man of wide vision and imaginative commonsense: 'He came of Westmorland and yeoman stock and remained a countryman all his life: perhaps it was an inherited instinct for doing things in their right season that gave him his flair for producing the idea for a new activity at the psychological moment when it could be most effectively undertaken.'[5] Ambrose Heal was a countryman *manqué*. Even Pick, chief prophet of Efficiency Style, had strong traces of the country-dweller's almost mystic attitude to nature and the land, a Wordsworthian sense of the unity of all living things, the harmony of man and nature.

'The vital and miraculous result is this', he told the DIA one day in Edinburgh, 'if we seek efficiency in production, which is industry, and if we seek efficiency in the product, which may be summed up in design, and if the efficiency that we seek leads us to a vast harmony of all things, then all things must become alive, part of the living world.'[6]

It is interesting how the English countrified tradition, which descends directly through the woodworkers, the potters and handweavers of the 1920s to the multifarious craft workshops of today, has also, less directly, perhaps, but just as deeply, affected the progress of design for British industry. Here the key figure, of course, is Gordon Russell who began as a designer in the Cotswold craft tradition but who, in the mid-1920s, made a gradual transition so that, by 1930, the furniture made in his factory in Broadway was almost all designed for quantity production. As Nikolaus Pevsner explained it:

'Gordon Russell suddenly turned modern . . . Speaking from personal memory,' (for Pevsner once worked with Gordon Russell), 'I would say that the furniture of between 1935 and the war, in its entirely contemporary, never mannered, and never showy style, equalled the best on the Continent, and its workmanship was more perfect than any I saw in the Continental shops I visited. The fact that the men who made these pieces, however much of the rough and preliminary work machines were gradually taking off them, were still the same men who had been the craftsmen of the 1920s bore fruit.'[7]

Pevsner liked, and understood, the essential Englishness of Gordon Russell's attitudes, the attitudes which sprang from his deep feelings for the countryside. (Utility was, after all, a kind of country furniture.) Gordon Russell's own designs, and the designs which he promoted, have a specially British quality of reticence, the virtue which Sedding once described so accurately as the 'imaginative handling of the commonplace'. This consistent understatement, a creative kind of modesty, is central to the British tradition of designing, stretching back to Philip Webb, the architect and friend of Morris, who always felt unhappy, he claimed, if his work looked anything but ordinary, and forward to the furniture designers of the 1950s (trained at the Royal College of Art by R.D.Russell) and the best of the industrial designers of today.

The British tradition, derived as it was from the Arts and Crafts movement of the late nineteenth century, was very much a workshop tradition of designing. By this I mean a process of design through making. Many of the most famous of the Arts and Crafts designers were themselves obsessive makers: one thinks of William Morris, his arms deep into the dye-vats; Sidney Barnsley selecting and then sawing his own timber for the furniture he made in his workshop in the Cotswolds. The whole period was a great time of rediscovery of technical skills and the artistic possibilities which sprang up from them. It was an age of excitement and delight both in the skills themselves, the sheer technical achievements, described in vivid detail in interminable essays by the designer-craftsmen of the time, and also in the leeway which these skills gave the designers in fulfilling what they saw to be their role within society, for setting the standards which they felt to be the right ones, for seeing through their theories of art and labour, the civilised relationship of work and life.

This implied a certain relaxation and open-mindedness. As Morris himself analysed it after his return from a visit to Edward Carpenter at Millthorpe:

> 'it seems to me that the real way to enjoy life is to accept all its necessary ordinary details and turn them into pleasures by taking an interest in them: whereas modern civilisation huddles them out of the way, has them done in a venal and slovenly manner till they become real drudgery which people can't help trying to avoid.'[8]

Joy in all life's simple things, and leisure to explore them, seemed to many of the followers of Morris essential components of a well-balanced human life. To work at their own pace and standard, free from outside pressures: this was seen not as an opting-out, a form of self-indulgence, but rather the reverse, a form of positive experiment, a pattern for society as it might one day be. No one took these ideas further, of course, than C.R.Ashbee, whose experiment in Campden, (thoroughly, though sadly, described in his own book *Craftmanship in Competitive Industry*), stretched the doctrine of creative work and useful leisure to what turned out to be its ultimate conclusion. His passionate belief in doing things as well as possible, whatever their status in the usual scale of values – mending a wall or designing a cathedral, singing a catch or delivering a treatise – came as a revelation to some of his Guild craftsmen (and, it must be said, remained a mystery to others). Its importance in British design history is obvious: not just in the emphasis which Ashbee places on workshop practicality, on closeness to materials, but also in his stress on the creative need for calmness, with the time to think, to judge, to discuss and to amend.

From the Arts and Crafts movement and on right through the century, to the 'nearness to need' preoccupations of the 1970s, one finds signs of the idea that the best design is the result of human carefulness. 'Every real work of art', wrote W.R.Lethaby, 'looks as if it was made by one person for another', and this concept of personal integrity, responsibility for all the detail of the making, which applies at its most literal to the single craft-made object, also had a wider meaning in relation to design for mass production, the areas in which the trained designer, as the century progressed, was increasingly involved. It has always been crucial to the British tradition for designers to be close to actual methods of production. John Sedding once made the very sensible pronouncement:

'Our manufactures must be of good materials and make. The designs must be good and well suited to the necessities of modern methods of production. Note, moreover, that it is not enough to get good designs, but the designer should, more or less, superintend their making at the factory. The designer should be part of the working staff of the factory, see his design take shape, and be consulted as required. We have had enough of studio designs.'[9]

This was very British thinking. Dated 1893.

The overlap of craft into machine production is, to me, one of the most unique and interesting aspects of the whole development of design in Britain. Only in Scandinavia has there been a comparable balance between workshop and factory designing. Gordon Russell, in a lecture which he gave in 1948 on the work of Royal Designers for Industry, listed a group of the designers in this category (of which he himself was, of course, a prime example). As well as Harold Stabler, designer of silver, glass, medals and enamels, for one-off as well as for quantity production, he mentioned Duncan Grant and Allan Walton, whose textile designs were first produced by hand to be translated into machine processes; and also Ethel Mairet, described as 'specialising in first-rate hand-woven and hand-spun textiles, but also interested in making experiments for machine weaving'. This was only the beginning of a tendency which was to become still more important in the early post-war period, as the workshop tradition was encouraged and expanded by the regimes at the COID and the Royal College of Art. In the next two decades the list of Royal Designers included such convinced hand-and-machine practitioners as Margaret Leischner, Marianne Straub, Enid Marx, David Mellor, Robert Welch.

This was 'doing-is-designing' philosophy in action. As Russell had explained it, it was, for instance, Eric Gill's close knowledge of each individual letter of the alphabet, a knowledge gained by actually drawing and cutting letters for years at a size far larger than ordinary type size, which made him such an efficient and sensitive designer of typefaces for the Monotype Corporation. Similarly, it was Robert Welch's training as a silversmith, his basic understanding of and feeling for the metal and the possibilities it allowed to the designer, which shaped his whole approach to the design of stainless steel and other industrial products in the 1950s.

It is, I think, this merging of hand and machine values, this fusion of technical expertise and deep instinctive feeling, the result of many years of craft connection, which gives British design a good deal of its conviction. Frank Pick, in the days of the Pick Council, once defined the national design character as:

'modest and not too grandiose in scale . . . not too logical in form . . . a reasonable compromise between beauty and utility, neither overstressing beauty till it degenerates into ornament, nor overstressing utility until it becomes bare and hard.'[10]

Not stark, but never sloppy; precise, but not inhuman. Up to a point, Frank Pick's description still rings true, even when applied to pure industrial designers. Through the long development of design for engineering, from the 1930s pioneers to Kenneth Grange and David Carter, British design has kept a certain sense of balance, a getting to the point, an avoidance of mere 'styling', which has its base, perhaps, in the old workshop practicalities and, over the years, has been a major source of strength.

The human quality in design, which Frank Pick noted, has always been a part of the British national character. Often this has meant not just good sense and moderation but individuality and strangeness and inventiveness. It has led to all those human quirks, the oddity and fantasy, affection and banter, with which design in Britain has been so much imbued. This was a tendency the Arts and Crafts made much of. Morris and Brother Rabbit; William De Morgan ('the whimsical De Morgan', as C.R.Ashbee called him), with his fantastic sequences of birds and beasts and fishes; Walter Crane, who so much loved the quaint and magical and childish, even dressing up his wife as a sunflower for a party: the Arts and Crafts were full of these inventions and surprises. They took up the motifs of the picture book and folk tale, the most beautiful example of which is the Baillie Scott commission, in 1898, to design a royal tree-house for the Crown Princess Marie of Romania in the woods on the family's summer estate. This house, a wooden cabin, was designed to be supported by a group of eight trees twenty-five feet above the ground. The Arts and Crafts delight in the *faux naïve* and fairytale, a childlike perspicacity and sense of wonder, comes over most consistently in the designs of Voysey. His work is, I think, an extraordinary instance of commercial application of a highly personal vision. In his book *Individuality* he lays great stress on personal development:

'Let us assume,' he says, 'that there is a beneficent and omnipotent controlling power, that is perfectly good and perfectly loving; and that our existence here is for the purpose of growing individual characters.'

He sees it as essential to the civilised community to preserve individual creativity and even individual idiosyncrasy in the face of advancing tendencies of standardisation and bureaucracy:

'. . . if we would train character and preserve individual responsibility, we must most jealously guard individualism. Especially in these days, when the state has degenerated into a machine for producing armies of officials, with volumes of rules and regulations stereotyped and settled to suit given conditions, which by the laws of Nature must be for ever changing and developing.'[11]

This individualism Voysey carried through not just in the design of his personal and changeable and somehow childlike houses, but also in the details of his furniture and ironwork; his use of homely symbols, like the ever-present heart; the birds and flowers entwining in the patterns of his textiles and his wallpapers, giving them a character so English (and so Voysey-like) it sometimes seems as if they verge on the surreal.

English individuality has only sometimes taken a form of ornate richness: as, for instance, in the breathtakingly complex, neo-Byzantine metalwork of Henry Wilson. It has usually had a much more everyday emphasis in which the originality consisted in a new interpretation of the normal things around us. Back again to William Morris and Morris's conviction that peasant art was the best and most *English* form of decorative art. There has been a strong tradition in British design thinking, from

Gimson's hay-rake stretchers to Keith Murray's famous beer-mugs, of sophisticated treatment of the basic equipment of ordinary living. There has also been a knowledgeable cultivation of basic English folk art, and especially the art of the fairground and the popular theatre. What was seen as the natural exuberance of folk art, the instinctive sense of pattern, the joyful uninhibited use of brightest colours, in some reckless combinations, delighted the designers of the 1920s in particular. One can see the influence in Lovat Fraser's textiles and in the Poole pottery of that same period. Concurrent was the widespread interest in puppeteering in the advanced design circles of the 1920s, and the highly-cultivated low-life habits of the era – the visits to the village pub, pursuit of local pastimes – which related to the theory, held by Eric Gill and others, that an artist or designer was an ordinary chap.

Enid Marx has been particularly keen on the folklorique. As recounted in the introduction to the catalogue of her retrospective exhibition in London in 1979, she very early on in her career began collecting examples of English popular ephemera: the chap books, broadsheets, pattern papers, toy theatre sheets, and so on. She also soon became intrigued with the continuing vitality of English popular decoration and craftwork: the Staffordshire pottery, the corn dollies, barge furniture, wrought-iron work and English inn signs, the images with which we feel so much at home that we have almost ceased to recognise their value. These themes recur not only in her work, for her textiles and her graphics are themselves ideal examples of traditional Englishness, but also in the books which she has written on the subject – *English Popular and Traditional Art*, in 1946; *English Popular Art*, in 1951.

English popular art has been so very much in favour among the design cognoscenti through the century not just on account of its sheer decorative qualities but also because of its intrinsic moral purity. Peasant art (and even savage art) was seen to be a good art, springing from the real and not the artificial values. Such artefacts as the painted gipsy wagon – the symbol of the freedom of the open road, as used by Augustus John and family – became, in design circles, the favourite exemplars of the human attributes of primitive designing, the exuberant directness so admired by design pundits. Even Frank Pick, chief-executive-to-be of London Transport, not perhaps the man most likely to fall for the charms of horse-drawn locomotion, could be heard extolling the humanity and honesty of caravans and hay-wains and happy barge-men's cabins. Said Pick, with feeling:

'The gipsy caravan has its close-set ribs and frame, notched and carved and painted with gay lines and dabs of colour, red or green or blue, on its yellow surface; the farmer's wain away in the far country is the same; the little cabin in the stern in which the barge-dweller lives is still bright and joyous.'

In contrast, he depicted the falsity of styling of the delivery van then in use by a large London store. The body of this van had an eccentric curve, not, judged Pick, because the curve followed necessarily from structure, but because the curve had been consciously sought as being odd and distinctive. He went on:

'It shows no structure at all, but is encased in shiny sombre green and bears on its smooth finished surfaces the name of its proud possessor in precise and gilded letters. Such is the difference between the individual seeking the great adventure of self-expression heedless of the goal of distinctiveness and the individual seeking after the goal of distinctiveness heedless of the great adventure.'[12]

Which came, in later years, to be seen as the distinction between the true industrial designer and the stylist.

The details of the English scene entranced not only Pick but many of his fellow-members of the DIA. The English landscape, both the countryside and townscape, was a passion to Clough Williams-Ellis, architect of fantasy and author of so many of the inter-war campaigns to save the face of the land from desecration. His quizzical, affectionate attitude to England, his love of the visual absurdities as well as the English scenic splendours, and his longing to preserve them, was, in its time, extremely influential. The same feeling of enchantment with the oddities of England can be glimpsed in the design work of Ravilious and Bawden in the 1920s and 1930s: Edward Bawden's tiles for Carter, Stabler, Adams, and mugs and jugs and bowls and urns for Wedgwood by Ravilious, with their Boat Race scenes and vistas of the crowds in Piccadilly, share this quality of quiet conviviality, this curiosity and pleasure at the passing scene. The feeling re-emerges at the Festival of Britain: the Lion and Unicorn Pavilion was full of it, a large-scale celebration, designed by Robert Goodden and R.D. Russell, of the British national character and British way of life which stressed, as well as British dignity and British doggedness, the national predilection for whimsy, eccentricity and a kind of gentle urge for self-congratulation. This was very much the impulse of the time, a hopeful era. When in 1948 Robin Darwin became Principal of the Royal College of Art, he made the wish that his forthcoming students should be literate, articulate, of broad intelligence, with minds that were 'amused and well-tempered'. The term well-tempered maybe seems a little baffling. The spirit of Ravilious was what I think he meant.

The idiosyncratic tendencies within the British design tradition, so superbly realised in Robert Goodden's silver in the early post-war period, had a later re-revival in the work of Gerald Benney and Louis Osman in the 1960s, the lavishness of which often verges on the jokey, and the flamboyantly eccentric work of Makepeace, whose furniture combines the strangely classical and freakish. The small craft-workshop movement of the past few years has provided a whole sequence of new individual statements. The Crafts Council has collected quite a number of the best ones. From the Crafts Council collection my own favourite is a teapot. A teapot by Jill Crowley. In fact a green-leaf teapot. A teapot or a cabbage? Or a comment on a nation which drinks tea and consumes cabbages? All that is certain is that when it comes to tea and cabbages, the national symbolism becomes tortuous indeed.

British design, at first sight so sane and simple, reveals an unexpected aspect of complexity the harder one looks at it. The rational and symbolic instincts co-exist to an astonishing degree. Look at Lethaby, for instance. What a man of rationality, a downright nuts-and-bolts man, with his practical reflections on viaducts and bicycles, and yet, at the same time, what a wild amazing thinker with his theories of egalitarian architectural symbolism. In his book *Architecture, Mysticism and Myth* (which Lethaby, half-jokingly, used to call 'the Cosmos'), he creates a whole new language of designing through a sequence of associative visual ideas: pavements like the sun, ceilings like the sky, labyrinths, and golden gates, the jewel-bearing tree; a literary language, with images from folklore, and dominated by the very symbol of creation. Some of his contemporaries wondered what to make of it. But others found it totally rewarding and inspiring. Robert Weir Schultz maintained that, for him, it opened up an undreamed-of world of romance in architecture, and May Morris, embroidery and jewellery designer, said that she had fallen on the book with much delight. Certainly, accumulative symbolism, layers of meaning, by the later 1890s were increasingly apparent in the metalwork and bookbindings, the textiles and the hangings of the more expressionist wing of Arts and Crafts.

The element of ecstasy should never be discounted in British design tradition. One way or another, it has always been recurring, onwards from Ruskin and 'All great Art is praise'.

First, the ecstasy of sheer creative possibilities: from John D.Sedding, 1886.
'By his divine craft the priest of form can fold in one the magic in nature and man's emotion – he can steal nature's seal and print it upon his work – he can put the glamour of the woods into his timber roofs or stone vaultings, can bring the might of the tall cliffs into his walls and fluted columns, can entice the soul of the tangled thicket into the mazes of his carved beaten work, can give to the temple of God such an air of religiousness – fill its recesses with such an air of mystery and stillness, that you get a strange thrill of expectancy as you enter, and say, involuntarily, "surely the Lord is in this place".'[13]

And also the ecstasy of personal creativity, the joy of actually making (ideally on a fresh and sunny morning in the springtime): from A.Romney Green, c.1946.
'There is no lovelier exercise in the world than that of planing up a figured oak board with a wooden jack plane . . . It taxes every muscle in your body from the soles of your feet to the tips of your fingers. The workshop is soon full of the acrid scent of the newly cut oak (or the aromatic scent of pine or cedar) as the shavings come, almost whistling, through the mouth of your plane and fall in foam about your feet.'[14]

And then the ecstasy of mastery of a technology, a feeling which developed from the Arts and Crafts preoccupation with skill and with technique towards the sense of glory in technology which seemed so to obsess the designers of the 1970s. This quotation comes from a cult book of that period, *Zen and the Art of Motor Cycle Maintenance*, quoted within another cult book of the 1970s, Dr Patrick Nuttgens' *Learning to Some Purpose*, 1977:
'if you have to choose among an infinite number of ways to put it together then the relation of the machine to you, and the relation of the machine and you to the rest of the world, has to be considered, because the selection from among many choices, the art of the work, is just as dependent upon your own mind and spirit as it is upon the material of the machine. That's why you need the peace of mind.'[15]

The spiritual and almost ludicrously practical; emotional and reticent, highminded, sentimental; the ornate and the symbolic and the plain and the straightforward; the mixture of radical and innovative urges with a deep conservatism: the contrasts of British design character are obvious, and have helped to shape its subtle individuality. But what is not so obvious, perhaps, yet fascinating – a trait which is, I think, peculiar to Britain and of very great importance to the national design story – is the way the individualism, almost always, is contained within the group, is exerted in a context of group aims, collective attitudes. This has always been the

16 (*opposite*)
'Tree of Life' vase in stoneware, with incised decoration,
made at St Ives by Bernard Leach, c.1950. The tree-of-
life was a recurring theme of Leach's and has an
interesting counterpart in the industrial pottery of the
World War II period (cf. Susie Cooper, no.136).
Leicestershire Museums.

British background of designing. There has always been a pattern of groups forming
and reforming, aims discussed, action plans made, papers read, committees meeting,
a man's world of bonhomie, of friendly, moderate efficiency, which has had great
influence on the whole history of design.

William Morris was, of course, the first and greatest exemplar of gregarious
designing. He began, as a young man, with the streak of amateurism which has
often been endearingly apparent in British design practice, by making some rough
sketches for a settle and some tables and chairs for the house in Red Lion Square
which he was sharing with Burne-Jones. These were constructed by a local carpenter.
On the panels of the high-backed settle, and the chairbacks, Dante Gabriel Rossetti,
another friend of Morris's, painted scenes of Sir Galahad and Dante. Morris then
designed a wardrobe which Burne-Jones decorated with figures from *The Prioress'
Tale* by Chaucer. When William Morris married and moved into Red House, the
house in the country which Philip Webb had designed for him, Webb also designed
furniture, brass candlesticks, grates, fire-irons and table glass (besides a gothic
wagon for touring round the countryside); Burne-Jones designed decorative stained-
glass windows; Morris himself designed embroideries and hangings, gradually
carried out by the ladies of his circle. These early exercises in collective creativity,
the idea of the value of the pool of expertise, which is indeed still with us, in modern
design practices, encouraged the formation, in 1861, of Morris, Marshall, Faulkner
& Company. The other partners were Webb, Burne-Jones, Rossetti and Ford
Madox Brown. The work they undertook, according to the first prospectus, was a
superior form of decoration, what would now be termed a co-ordinated interior
design service: they offered to carry out and supervise whole schemes involving wall
paintings, decoration, stained glass, metalwork and jewellery, sculpture, embroidery
and all kinds of furniture for houses and for churches 'at the smallest possible
expense'. As it turned out, the expense was sometimes great, and even then the
profits could often be derisory. The motivation of Morris, Marshall, Faulkner & Co.
was not, needless to say, primarily commercial. It was a venture in which the spirit
of camaraderie was stronger than the interest in marketing, a scale of values
characteristically English, with results which I shall hope to follow through.

William Morris was the centre of a network of design-reforming groups in the
late nineteenth century. The Society for the Preservation of Ancient Buildings,
founded in 1877; the Art Workers' Guild, in 1884; the Arts and Crafts Exhibition
Society, in 1888. Not surprisingly, perhaps, since these societies had many members
in common – a nucleus of architects and craftsmen, painters and sculptors of a
progressive, though sociable, mien – the atmosphere within them was really very
similar: sincerity, good comradeship (remarked on by May Morris), gentlemanliness,
an earnest form of jocularity. Lethaby described it nicely, referring to his own
acceptance into this charmed circle, and his attendance at the weekly meetings of
the SPAB:

'It was Gimson who introduced me to the Society and the circle in 1891. For a
time – a great time to me – we attended meetings, from 5 to 7, and then went
across the Strand to Gatti's for an evening meal: Morris often, Webb always, and
two or three of a number of younger lesser people, Gimson, Emery Walker,
Sydney Cockerell, Detmar Blow and myself; here were stories, jokes, real talk.

17
'Ticker Tape' printed furnishing fabric designed by
Lucienne Day for Heal Fabrics, 1954. A very successful
post-Festival of Britain pattern (comparable with
Lucienne Day's more well-known 'Calyx', no.165), with
a subtle use of that favourite designer's colour of the
period, Thames Green. Whitworth Art Gallery,
University of Manchester.

18
'Flamingo' furnishing cotton designed by Tibor Reich
and manufactured by Tibor, 1957. The 'Fotexturprint'
technique used in arriving at the pattern much impressed
the judges at the Council of Industrial Design and the
fabric was included in the first of the Design Centre
Awards. Tibor Reich.

19
'Five' printed linen and cotton furnishing fabric designed
by Shirley Craven for Hull Traders, 1966. Whitworth
Art Gallery, University of Manchester.

20
'Shape' printed furnishing cotton designed by Shirley
Craven for Hull Traders, 1964. Whitworth Art Gallery.
University of Manchester.

21
'Reciprocation' printed furnishing cotton designed by
Barbara Brown for Heal Fabrics, 1963. Whitworth Art
Gallery, University of Manchester.

22
'Glenaffric Check' woven furnishing fabric designed by
Peter Simpson for Donald Brothers, 1962. Peter Simpson.

23
Rag rug, hand-dyed and hand-woven by John
Hinchcliffe, 1977. The use of traditional techniques to
new effect: a classic product of the workshop revival of
the 1970s. Private collection.

24
'Maze' printed cotton designed by Hans Tisdall for
Tamesa Fabrics, 1978. A large-scale design, but softer in
character than the big, brash textiles of the 1960s, more
in keeping with the new vernacular buildings of the
period. Tamesa Fabrics.

25 and 26
Woven Irish linen for a range of kitchen textiles
developed by the hand-weavers Roger Oates and Fay
Morgan for large-scale production by David Mellor,
1981. Roger Oates.

27
Cabinet with ebony, holly and dyed beech veneer, 1972,
designed by Michael Gurney, then a student at the
Royal College of Art. (He died tragically young in that
same year.) A spectacular piece, prophetic both of the
considerable revival of hand-made furniture later in the
decade, and also the reawakened interest in Oriental art
and design. College collection, Royal College of Art.

28
The Crayonne 'Input' range, first launched in 1973 by
Airfix Plastics and Conran Associates: the first serious
attempt to apply high-design principles to everyday
household plastics, the forerunner of many similar
collections, and a long-term commercial success. Conran
Associates.

There was a kindly old waiter from North Italy whom we call Ticino, who smiled at us like a host.'[16]

There was something very schoolboyish about these Arts and Crafts groups. The Art Workers' Guild, although very shy in public, almost pathologically nervous of publicity, was different in private, full of badinage and boisterousness. *The Art Workers' Guild* history, written by H.J.L.Massé in 1935, year of the Guild's half-century, has many references to past Art Workers' Guild festivities and the good-natured chaff and banter these engendered. Some became the stuff of legend. Reginald Blomfield, in his memoirs, mentions the Shrovetide revels of 1892, the year that William Morris was in the chair. Wrote Blomfield:

'George Frampton, who, whatever his merits as a sculptor, possessed a most droll humour, acted the little Blondel donkey, with somebody else behind, George being the head. I was bowled over in cock-fighting by T.R.Spence, architect, while E.P.Warren, architect, an old friend of mine, watched us with solemn and immovable dignity. Many years later Frampton and I were able to help Spence at the Royal Academy.'[17]

The point I want to make is not just that many major designers of the day were good at being silly, but – a feeling emphasised by Blomfield's final sentence, in which he talks of helping Spence at the Academy – that collective loyalty, the sense of shared experience, between many of the leaders of design in that far-off period, created a strong code, almost a kind of a freemasonry, which, it could be argued, has continued to exist.

The Arts and Crafts movement was in fact a whole succession of groups within groups. For instance, the young architect-designers of Shaw's office (where, once again, the horseplay was very much in evidence): Lethaby, Mervyn Macartney, Edward Prior, Robert Weir Schultz and Sidney Barnsley; the young architect-designers who worked with John D.Sedding: Ernest Barnsley, Henry Wilson, Ernest Gimson, Alfred Powell, John Paul Cooper. These groups split off and reassembled through the period. Some of the members later re-met in the Cotswolds. But earlier, in 1890, five of these designers – Gimson, Lethaby, Blomfield, Macartney, Sidney Barnsley – had joined in setting up a small experimental workshop, Kenton & Co., in Bedford Row, in London. They designed the furniture and employed professional craftsmen who made it up for them. They enjoyed themselves immensely and were totally unbusinesslike:

'We made no attempt', wrote Blomfield, 'to interfere with each other's idiosyncrasies. Lethaby's and Gimson's inventions ran to simple designs of admirable form in oak. I recollect a mirror frame, rather Persian in design, inlaid with mother-of-pearl, by Sidney Barnsley and much admired by Leighton. Macartney followed the elegant motives of the eighteenth century, and I indulged myself in solid rosewood.'[18]

Kenton & Co., which was in effect a forerunner of the co-operative craft workshops of the 1970s, in that the designers, although sharing all the overheads, were working independently, closed down two years later. Though they had hardly hoped to, they had not made a profit, and divided up the furniture among themselves to repay their original capital investment. Mostly they chose their own designs. But Lethaby selected an oak cabinet by Blomfield with an inlaid pattern of rabbits eating lettuce.

The main motive of Kenton & Co. had been the pleasure of the founding partners. Design for entertainment. This was just as true of the Omega Workshops, although the style of product was altogether different. The Omega was founded in 1913 by Roger Fry, the art critic and painter and, incidentally, in years gone by, a friend of Ashbee's, though Fry had never had the same belief in craftsmanship. Indeed, the Omega in a sense was anti-craftsmanship: Fry was apt to buy a Dryad chair and paint it red (*Venetian* red, the favoured colour of the Omega). The idea of the Omega was a gathering of artists – Fry himself, Duncan Grant, Vanessa Bell and others – aiming to express their individual sensibility through the decoration of normal household objects, the cups, the chairs, the tables people often take for granted. It was a group project, though the group around the Omega seemed particularly prone to upheavals and reversals; it was, in a way, the working-out of Fry's own theory that 'the greatest art has always been communal, the expression – in highly individualised ways no doubt – of common aspirations and ideals'.[19] Its spirit of experiment reminds one of the joie de vivre, and the naivety, of Morris & Co. at the beginning; and in its iconoclastic urges, its will to shatter the complacency and dullness of the capitalist manufactured product by showing an alternative set of design values, it was, as it turned out, an extraordinary foretaste of the anarchic design movement of today.

The Design and Industries Association, meanwhile, also had its eye on British chairs and English teapots. But it had a relatively steady bourgeois theory, viz. that if a thing were unaffectedly made to fulfil its purpose thoroughly, then it would be good art: a very reasonable surmise. The DIA in those days, in the years between the Wars, was the chief, indeed the only, design group of any substance. 'It was not', wrote John Gloag once, 'a society for Art twaddle'. Art, or any other, twaddle was not its line at all. The DIA was supremely conscientious; as much, if not more so, than the Arts and Crafts societies which, in a sense, gave birth to it and from which it drew so many of its members. It was a group with admirable fixity of purpose. As the Yearbook for 1926 so well expressed it: 'Fashion ebbs and flows, but DIA principles remain true'. Like the Arts and Crafts societies before it, it had its own built-in hierarchy: first W.R.Lethaby became the father figure, revered theorist and spokesman, and then Frank Pick took over. Ranged round them were the henchmen – the Heals, the Harry Peaches, the Curwens and the Stablers – good-natured men of principle, their hearts in the right place. The DIA, of course, had its own robust code of honour, and shared the Arts and Crafts distaste for self-publicity. Like the Arts and Crafts, as well, it had its private jokes, its banter, its rather unremitting hail-fellow-well-met atmosphere. Even more, perhaps, than Arts and Crafts, the DIA mid-period, the tucket-sounding years of the 1920s and 1930s, exudes the tweedy sense of well-meaning masculinity, the predilection for the predictable and clubbable, which lasted so long in British design life.

This is not to say that the design groups were immovable. Though set in their ways, the emphasis within them shifted quite considerably according to the period. In the early years of the Arts and Crafts societies, painters and sculptors, besides architects and craftsmen, were included in the grouping. This was the whole intention: the Art Workers' Guild and the Art and Crafts Exhibition Society were set up to establish a common ground between the fine artist and the craftsman: 'an honest and sincere attempt', as Blomfield put it, 'to find a common standpoint from which all the graphic and plastic arts and crafts should be approached'.[20] The DIA evinced a comparable catholicity: its membership, though hardly bursting at the seams with sculptors, covered a very broad spectrum of designing and drew in other members from ancillary professions, from writing, journalism and even the more reputable advertising agencies, as well as the captains of industry which it cultivated with enormous assiduity. During the 1930s the groupings changed again, not least with the foundation of the Society of Industrial Artists, the professional society, in 1930. But the atmosphere remained, it seems, astonishingly constant. The design groups were still very much a band of brothers. Here is James Holland, in his Jubilee history of the SIA, describing those early scenes of camaraderie:

'the embryo Society amounted to a select group of artists, designers and craftsmen – later becoming several groups – meeting regularly and convivially, to discuss the pursuit of their stated aims and to listen to lectures and discourses by colleagues and guest speakers. My earliest personal recollection of encountering the SIA is of a friendly evening of talk, darts and bitter in a south London pub, a tweedy, pipe-smoking occasion much in keeping with the character of that pre-war decade'.[21]

One important feature of the SIA in those days was its link, once again, to the fine artists. In the 1930s, according to James Holland's perspicacious Jubilee analysis, a quite surprising number of fine artists were actively involved in the Society's working structure. In 1932–3, Paul Nash was President; Frank Dobson, Graham Sutherland and Allan Walton, among other well-known artists, were members of the Council. Partly, this reflected an ideal: the new conception of the potential role of the artist in relation to machine production, as the theories of the Bauhaus gradually percolated through to Britain. (It was, wrote Paul Nash in 1932, in a mood of some intoxication, the duty of the artist to invade the house as a designer in materials ranging from 'stone, paper, glass, steel, wood, cardboard, rubber, leather, fabrics and endless synthetic and artificial patent compositions',[22] and he foresaw that 'the professional artist of the future would be a professional designer'.[23]) But as well as an ideal, the feeling for the merging of art into design reflected a reality: the 1930s were becoming a great period for patronage, and artists were employed (as designers) quite consistently by such entrepreneurs as Frank Pick at London Transport, Jack Beddington at Shell, Stephen Tallents at the GPO and Tom Heron of Cresta. There were famous 1930s projects like the Foley range of pottery designed by artists (Paul Nash in fact was one of them); and Edinburgh Weavers' collection of textiles commissioned from painters (another enterprise with which Paul Nash had been connected). The proximity of design groups and fine artists in the 1930s, a time when design education theories were surfacing, encouraged the conviction that training for designers should be carried out in art-orientated schools and colleges: a belief which only now is beginning to be questioned.

In the 1930s, the links were also very architectural. The design world and the architects were close together because, in many cases, the designers *were* the architects. The few actual industrial designers of the period, designers edging into such areas as furniture, ceramics, glass and engineering – Wells Coates, Serge Chermayeff, Robert Gooden, R.D. Russell, Jack Howe, Keith Murray – were all architects by training. Many of the members of the design groups proper, the DIA and SIA, had strong affiliations with the progressive architectural group practices, Tecton for instance, and also with the MARS group. The ex-Bauhaus architects Walter Gropius and Marcel Breuer arrived in London in the mid-1930s, refugees from Nazi Germany. A home was offered to them by Jack Pritchard at Lawn Road Flats in Hampstead. This building, completed in 1934, had been designed for Jack and Molly Pritchard by Wells Coates, and it is now regarded as a classic of its period, one of the few landmarks of the British Modern Movement. The social centre of Lawn Road was the Isobar, which Breuer had designed, and to which naturally gravitated architects, designers and what counted as the international modernists of England.

The groupings within groupings, the complex interweavings, of British design history are nowhere more apparent than in the Faculty of Royal Designers for Industry, which was set up by the Royal Society of Arts in 1936. This relatively small and élite body of designers, self-elected, from quite varied design disciplines, astonishingly English in its structure and its attitudes, forms a kind of microcosm of the whole design profession. In 1948, twelve years after it was founded, Gordon Russell gave a paper, 'The Work of the Royal Designers for Industry', analysing in most fascinating detail the major design groupings, as they then appeared. What is striking is not just the sheer profusion, the multiple approaches to industrial designing, but the energy and zest for corporate activities among many of the Royal Designers of that period. He lists the architectural group within the Faculty, the many RDIs in architectural practice. He lists the RDIs who, at the same time, are fine artists – painters, etchers or lithographers – and puts a special emphasis upon the stage designers, Anna Zinkeisen, Gordon Craig and Laurence Irving. He defines the exhibitions group (Gardner, Gray, Coates, Gordon Russell himself); the typographic group (Meynell, J.H.Mason, Percy Delf Smith); the all-round-designers group (Robert Goodden, Harold Stabler); the more specialist furniture and radio designers (Ambrose Heal, Wells Coates again and R.D.Russell, Gordon Russell's brother). He contrasts the pure engineering group (Sir Geoffrey de Havilland, Barnes Wallis and Charles Nicholson) with the more craft-minded hand-to-machine designers (Duncan Grant, Allan Walton, Ethel Mairet, Robert Goodden, and two past Royal Designers, James Hogan, glass designer, and Eric Gill, described by Gordon Russell as 'the outstanding figure of this class'). He goes on to consider the designer-manufacturer (RDIs like Allan Walton, Susie Cooper) and the designer-manufacturer-and-shopkeeper (of which the one example he can find is Ambrose Heal). There are other groups to come. The design directors' group: Reco Capey of Yardleys, Ashley Havinden of Crawfords, A.B.Read of Troughton and Young Lighting. The design-in-education group. The list of Royal Designers who sit on myriad design advisory committees (this group totals seventeen, almost as much as half the Faculty). Many of the RDIs belong in two or three compartments, interconnecting to outside design strongholds. No less than ten had been involved at one time or another, Gordon Russell notes with awe, in design commissions from Frank Pick at London Transport; several had been working under the aegis of the Utility Furniture Design Panel (of which Gordon Russell himself had been the Chairman). In this early post-war period, the network of designers, as Gordon

Russell points out with immense pleasure – for networks suited Gordon Russell – was considerable. Milner Gray, SIA President, was a Royal Designer. Gordon Russell, at the time of his paper, was both Master of the Faculty and Director of the Council of Industrial Design.

Gordon Russell had great hopes, the hopes which we have seen before among reformers of design in Britain, of the moral efficacy of designing, the designer's role in helping to regenerate the nation. He ended his paper on the Royal Designers, touchingly, on a note of highest visionary fervour, seeing design as one of the prime factors in the post-war revival of the country:

> 'I think you will agree with me', he said, 'when I say that one would be optimistic indeed to believe that wars lead to an improvement in manners. The exact opposite is the case. Over great areas of the world we find today the most elementary rules of courtesy flouted and, not unnaturally, human relationships do not survive the strain. The standard of industrial design in a country is one of the visible signs of its standard of manners and of its general approach to life. Never was it so important to hold fast to real values. Here we are determined that the Faculty shall play its part, albeit a very small one, in the great revolution we are witnessing.'[24]

In 1951, year of the Festival of Britain, many of these heartfelt hopes were still extant. The Festival, although perhaps one should not view it as the sign of a new civilisation evolving, was certainly a very effective morale-booster in that bleak period of post-war austerity and a quite enormous stimulus for innovation in architecture and design. The artistic control of the whole Festival, from the use of the site to the selection of the teaspoons, involving a hundred architects and designers, working in groups and sub-groups, was an extraordinary exercise in teamwork which confirmed the British talent for corporate designing. One also gathers, from the stream of reminiscence which has since then poured from those who took part in the Festival (the Festival has now acquired an element of folklore), that, for the designers, it was not just very valuable experience, put to good use later, but the most enormous fun. It was a perfect period for the groupings and regroupings which have occurred so rhythmically in British design history. A good many Royal Designers were designers for the Festival: Hugh Casson RDI was architectural Director. Many Festival designers had also been recruited for the Royal College of Art, just then beginning in its new incarnation under Robin Darwin. Festival figures reassembled in new guises: Professor Sir Hugh Casson; Professor Robert Goodden; Professor R.D.Russell; Professor Misha Black.

Possibly by then it had just become a habit. But one senses that the impulse towards corporate designing is more deeply allied to British character and outlook, and the post-war growth of multi-talent design offices has not been unrelated, although it has become increasingly less purist, to the joy in camaraderie of early design periods. The idea of working groups of artists and designers, complementary in talents, who enjoyed each other's company, has been so very central to the national tradition – from Morris, Marshall, Faulkner & Co. onward – that it does not need much stretch of the imagination to connect this through to the latter-day design groups. Design Research Unit was really the first of the professional large-scale design consultancies, formed in 1942, and drawing on the skills, in its early years, of the designers Milner Gray and Misha Black and Norbert Dutton, architects Frederick Gibberd and Sadie Speight, the structural engineer Felix Samuely, with Herbert Read as the Director. DRU explained its arguments for a group practice in an early leaflet:

> 'Like every aspect of modern industry, design should be a co-operative activity, and the function of DRU is to focus on every project it undertakes the combined knowledge and experience of several creative minds since it believes that only by pooling the talents of a team of designers is it possible to offer a service capable of meeting every demand from the wide and varied field of present-day activity.'[25]

The pool of talent theory has had an immense influence, since then, on the development of British design practice: there are dozens of examples in the post-war period of which the most convincing is Pentagram, perhaps.

British designing, a bit like British cooking, has absorbed a lot of foreign influences through the ages: assimilated them and created something new, and often in the end intensely British. The DIA, for instance, founded on the model of the Deutscher Werkbund, the German design pressure group, emerged very far from German, somehow almost doubly English. The original foreign influence, absorbed, made something different. Frank Pick, in 1930, much admired design in Denmark, the consistent design standards, on the large scale and in detail, in the streets of Copenhagen; this very much affected his London Transport policy, but Frank Pick's way of doing things remained completely British. British designers were receptive to the influence of both the USA and Scandinavia in the 1950s, Germany and, to some extent, Italy as well during the 1960s; and yet these were decades in which national design, far from being swamped, was actually strengthening. One could argue that this propensity towards design influence from abroad implies a marked degree of national tolerance and confidence. It can perhaps be seen as the natural extension of the British group tradition, the whole, large, settled structure of designing in this country, and related to the relative ease with which designers from abroad, in particular the many refugees from Europe in the 1930s, were absorbed not just into the professional design groups but also the whole hierarchy of design in Britain.

The coherence and conviction of design in Britain, as well as allowing the absorption of outside influence, has worked the other way: from inside outwards. The theories and the actual artefacts of Arts and Crafts made an extraordinary impact all through Europe and, as Pevsner pointed out so long ago, the reverberations from this period continued. The DIA delight in simple things fit for their purposes – farm implements and garden tools and sports equipment, from the golf club to the ultra-functional croquet mallet – was a source of fascination to many Scandinavians early in the 1930s and certainly encouraged the special design tendencies, the mixture of efficiency style and artful homeliness, in Swedish industrial design as it developed. The British Design Council, of course, has been the model for innumerable international design organisations, and the post-war British educational system for designers has, in scope and in ambition, been a source of wonder, much the most highly-developed in the world. The attributes, the virtues, of design in Britain have been coming under a new and intense scrutiny as British design services themselves have been exported with very great success. But there are few surprises. The qualities which make British design services covetable – so much so that some consultancies now claim that they are doing half their work away from Britain – are the traits which for so many years have been totally familiar: moderation, efficient, lucid thinking, commonsense.

And yet, has moderation been as far as we could get? Has moderation, in fact, been absolutely beneficial? Or have the obvious virtues of the national tradition, the honesty, the reticence, the care and equanimity, in fact, in some respects, almost been a liability? In the past few years – a major turning-point, it seems, in British design history, with many long-held values beginning to be challenged, and many old-established ways of doing things dismantled – much attention has been focused on the whole design tradition. It was obviously in many ways a generous tradition; there was a great deal which it encouraged and included. But doubts have been accumulating: was its tolerance so total? In fact hasn't there been also quite a lot which it shut out?

Certainly, through the years, its qualities of human niceness, relaxation, wit and whimsy, leisure and repose, have militated against rigorous professionalism. Professionalism has been a little suspect in the British tradition of designing. There has always been a certain nervousness of overdoing things, a gentlemanly horror of being seen to go too far. Frank Pick, for instance, criticised the lack of human quality in German design of the World War I period. He related how Professor Neumann of the Deutscher Werkbund urged the German architects 'to seize upon the house and create it in a German style . . . I remember reading once upon a time,' Pick added, 'how the colour of the cat was included in the prescription for a German home'.[26] His Art Workers' Guild audience would have seen this as preposterous: the colour of the cat could never be prescribed in Britain. It was totally against the British design ethos, then or later; the easy-going, civilised, comfortable, convivial, humorous, half-amateurish outlook on designing which has sometimes resulted in that British self-indulgence of designing rather less for one's clients than one's peers.

Certainly, too, the streak of cosy insularity in the British design movement made it terribly suspicious of anything it saw as even faintly strange and foreign. The room which E.W.Godwin designed in 1884 for Oscar Wilde fell well within this category: this was Anglo-Japanese in style, bare white and grey; the sparse furniture was white, except for one red lampshade. Walter Crane, the epitome of Englishness, denounced it, in the *Daily News*, as 'needlessly Spartan – there was a hair-shirt vigour about it opposed to all geniality and prandial humours'.[27] The English country background to the Arts and Crafts, the sense of fellowship, the love of the familiar and natural and wholesome, which brought about so much that was creative in that period, also led to an undoubted nervousness of novelty, amounting to a kind of a stick-in-the-mud quality, which lasted for many decades. This, together with the tendency for William Morris worship, was ridiculed quite sharply by Sir Lawrence Weaver in his introduction to the DIA Yearbook in 1927:

> 'No one is heard in disrespect of William Morris fabrics or tapestries or type. These things are English: they come from Hammersmith and Merton (where Lord Nelson abode) and had the flavouring name of Kelmscott. But Munich – à bas les Boches!'

A bas les Boches indeed. The traditions of the workshop, which had so much dominated the British design movement, the cult of works of art made by one human for another, the whole stress on individuality, the quirks and oddnesses which seemed to make the life of England very much worth living, meant that British design leaders of the 1920s and 1930s found international rationalism difficult to stomach: robot modernism, as John Gloag crossly called it.

'It is', wrote Philip Morton Shand in 1930, 'a melancholy and humiliating confession for an Englishman to make that the great movement towards standardisation of design in terms of functional fitness, to which the genius of the German people is now applying itself, should find no echo in the country which has initiated the Industrial Age. But it has to be candidly admitted that no nation has more stubbornly resisted rationalisation in industry: To none – not even the French – are standardisation and mass production more abhorrent.'[28]

Although Philip Morton Shand over-dramatised the problem, and the rationalist movement did make certain inroads into Britain by the middle of the 1930s, there was still something about it which made the British anxious. When it came, the British Modern Movement was a mild one. Rationalism, in its strictest form, was, simply, just not British: it contravened too much in our tradition of designing, the build-up of a deep feeling, the associationism.

It has always been intriguing how British design tradition, so positive in some ways, is so negative in others; progressive, but also so inbred and so conservative; receptive and yet in some ways curiously stubborn; welcoming and yet ironically prone to exclusivity. Its virtues almost always seem to have another side to them. The sturdy masculinity, in many ways so admirable, to which one can attribute the conviction and the vigour, the congeniality, of much of Arts and Crafts designing, was remarkably successful (albeit quite unconsciously) in setting up a pattern of anti-feminism within the British tradition in designing, of which there are still traces. The male-dominated world of Arts and Crafts has been exhaustively, and chillingly, described in Anthea Callan's *Angel in the Studio*. In the gathering of confrères, the women are irrelevant: the social pattern so stalwartly established in the Art Workers' revelries (the 'Eve-less Paradise' depicted by May Morris) extended to, for instance, the SPAB in Gatti's, the SIA pipe-smoking tweedily in the Cock Tavern. A pattern which, while not actually hostile towards woman, has scarcely been encouraging, and partially explains the considerable imbalance within the design profession even now.

British design is not much good at the erotic. Perhaps this is because of its early sense of purity, its aura of self-conscious bonhomie resulting in an attitude to women one can only term as puerile; in any case, eroticism has not featured greatly in the national tradition. Indeed, from time to time, it has seemed positively scaring. The erotic connotations of *art nouveau*, especially, left British commentators in a state of some confusion. 'Shows symptoms of pronounced disease',[29] as Lewis F.Day muttered, at the sight of *art nouveau* in October 1900. 'The majority of the exhibits were not only crude but meaningless', wrote Arthur Liberty in 1909, reporting on a visit to an exhibition of *art nouveau* paintings and drawings in Budapest: 'Nearly all the few clever ones were either obtrusively revolting in subject . . . or else erotic imaginings of morbid brains depicted with a mastery of technique only too wickedly perfect.'[30] In the clean, fresh atmosphere of mainstream British thinking, even the Glasgow School designers seemed too strange and esoteric: a reaction one might criticise as rather unimaginative. For it must be faced that in their long pursuit of sturdiness and plainness (both qualities quite simply seen as tantamount to goodness), the British have from time to time been very narrow-minded. They have shown, for instance, very little feeling for the glamorous: significantly, Eileen Gray, who had great sense of glamour, spent much of her career working outside Britain. There has also been consistent British mistrust of sheer brilliance which perhaps, in retrospect, has not been altogether wise.

British design has lacked a certain sense of stylishness. Again, this was a conscious rejection, going back to the Arts and Crafts ideals of basic honesty. 'Avoid', said Lethaby, 'the false smiles of the sham styles'. Avoiding the false smiles has had some curious effects, like the falling over backwards in the almost manically modern-minded 1950s to pour scorn on the creative neo-Georgian of the 1920s (a style the DIA had then, ironically, approved of). Only now has the design world started saying yes to Lutyens. Fixity of purpose; or shutting out of influence which might have been of value? Though there is no final answer, it does seem very likely that honesty and truthfulness cannot go on for ever, that the cult of the commonplace has rather overreached itself: at least in design markets in which fashion is an element. British design indubitably lacks sophistication beside, say, the very best Italian furniture today.

Anarchy is something else at which the British have not been too expert. This is not just a case of commonsense and sanity; for British design has had its mystics and its freaks. But the tenor has been more assimilative than rejective; the British have not had a lot of truck with the debunkers. No Studio Alchymia; no equivalent of Ettore Sottsass. Few anarchic revolutions: anyway not many yet.

The British tradition on the whole has been much gentler. The ideals which have formed it, though radical in some ways, have been calmer and more kindly. The reforming ideas, developed with such consistency from Ruskin, Morris, Lethaby to Pick and Gordon Russell, are intensely visionary and also deeply human. They have sprung from a real love of English countryside and British people. They show a strength of purpose, a generosity and an imaginative fervour which one cannot help admiring. And yet one also senses that this moralistic bias, the idea of basic rightness in designing, the conception of the designer as reformer, the bearer of the message, the bringer of the light, has set up a whole sequence of most complex inhibitions, the dangers of which are maybe only now being realised, and has started long debates about the values and the future of the British tradition of design.

It seems a fair conjecture that the highly moralistic, and indeed, at the beginning, anti-capitalist, leanings of British design, the whole intense, elaborate, self-righteous philosophy, has resulted in what one might call a lack of gumption in tackling modern problems of design for the world markets. An instinctive distrust of publicity and marketing; even a lingering suspicion of commerce. It also seems likely that the British group tradition, the networks of designing, the hierarchic patterns, have encouraged a pleasant, but insidious, complacency, a group tendency to make the best of things and not to question the generally accepted attitudes and values. 'We keep jogging along in our quiet way', as the DIA once mentioned in an early Yearbook. How charming, modest, British. But, also, how self-satisfied. Did they ever ask themselves, jogging towards what?

In the succeeding chapters of this book I shall be attempting to take a closer look at the evolution of the British tradition, period by period, and along the route from homeliness to eccentricity, from 1880s fantasy to 1980s deadpan, from conviviality to ecstasy, to outline the main tendencies within design élitism over the past century and to trace through the sequence of events which has, it now appears, resulted in the kind of crisis of identity, both personal and national, with which the design profession is confronted.

It is easy to see, from just a quick glance through these pages, that the British tradition, as it has built up over this long period, has been based on individual flair and creativity. It is a tradition, in a way, of star performers: such innovative talents as, in the early period, E.W.Godwin and Christopher Dresser; Morris and De Morgan; Ashbee, Voysey, Gimson, Mackintosh and many others working in the individualistic manner of the Arts and Crafts. The Arts and Crafts movement was indeed mainly responsible for the whole principle of designer-as-individual, designer as maverick, licensed to set up in opposition to society: the role filled in the years between the two World Wars by Eric Gill and also, less ostentatiously, by Bernard Leach. In the 1930s, under influence from the United States, designers in Britain became very nearly superstars: Wells Coates, Bernard, Chermayeff, were almost design idols. And in the post-war period, encouraged by the early promotional policies of the COID and by the design journalism of that period, the idea of the designer's individual contribution came across to a wide public. No wonder that designers now feel a little baffled. Over the past decade, the pattern has much altered. The designer-as-individual is less convincing. Design offices are larger, with new emphasis on teamwork. Design commissions too are much bigger and more complex. The tradition of personal design patronage is weakening in an era of industrial rationalisation, takeover and merger. Innovation is rarer, risks are much less often feasible; there is a general atmosphere of drawing-in, of caution, which designers, not unnaturally, find disorientating. In this context it is maybe too early to discern whether the craft revival of the past few years, the move back to the individual workshop, is important, a meaningful new phase of the tradition of personal experiment, or just an aberration. In the climate of the times it is an unexpected and, one may well find, an over-optimistic trend.

The other obvious question which emerges from these pages, the sequence of design from William Morris to Pentagram, is just how far a national style continues to be valid. Looking through the illustrations, one must admit the Britishness, strong in the first three sections, up as far as 1930, from then on becomes progressively more watered-down, more modified. The designs which illustrate the 1960s and the 1970s, though still I think quite characteristically British, are gradually acquiring internationalist identity. Is this, one has to wonder, good, bad, or just inevitable? Will there *be* British design by the early 1990s? Or, in years to come, will the national tradition almost cease to have any relevance at all?

References

[1] Quoted Christian Barman: *The Man Who Built London Transport: A Biography of Frank Pick* (Newton Abbot, David & Charles, 1979)

[2] W.R.Lethaby: *Form in Civilisation: Collected Papers on Art and Labour* (London, Oxford University Press, 1922)

[3] Quoted J.D.Sedding: 'Our Arts and Handicrafts,' paper read at Liverpool Art Congress, 1888, and reprinted in *Art and Handicraft* (London, Kegan Paul, Trench, Trubner & Co., 1893)

[4] Misha Black: 'Fitness for What Purpose?' Article in *Design* magazine, January 1974

[5] Hamilton Temple Smith: 'The History of the DIA: The Early Years.' Article in *Design for Today*, May 1935, reprinted in *DIA Yearbook* 1975

[6] 1Quoted Christian Barman: *The Man who Built London Transport*, ibid.

[7] Nikolaus Pevsner: 'Gordon Russell'. Article in *Architectural Review*, CXXXII, 1962

[8] Quoted Philip Henderson: *William Morris, his life, work and friends* (London, Thames and Hudson, 1967)

[9] J.D.Sedding: 'Our Arts and Handicrafts', ibid.

[10] Quoted Christian Barman: *The Man Who Built London Transport*, ibid.

[11] C.F.A.Voysey: *Individuality* (London, Chapman and Hall, 1915)

[12] Quoted Christian Barman: *The Man Who Built London Transport*, ibid.

[13] J.D.Sedding: 'Religion and Art,' paper read at Portsmouth Church Congress, 1886, and reprinted in *Art and Handicraft*, ibid.

[14] A.Romney Green: fragment of autobiography (unpublished), in MS collection of the Victoria and Albert Museum

[15] Quoted Dr Patrick Nuttgens: *Learning to Some Purpose* (London, Society of Industrial Artists and Designers, 1977)

[16] W.R.Lethaby: 'Ernest Gimson's London Days', chapter in *Ernest Gimson, His Life and Work* (Stratford-upon-Avon, Shakespeare Head Press, 1924)

[17] Sir Reginald Blomfield: *Memoirs of an Architect* (London, Macmillan, 1932)

[18] Sir Reginald Blomfield: *Memoirs of an Architect*, ibid.

[19] Roger Fry: *Vision and Design* (London, Chatto & Windus, 1920)

[20] Sir Reginald Blomfield: *Memoirs of an Architect*, ibid.

[21] James Holland: *Minerva at Fifty: The Jubilee History of the SIAD, 1930 to 1980* (Westerham, Hurstwood Publications, 1980)

[22] Paul Nash: 'The Artist in the House'. Article in *The Listener*, 16 March 1932

[23] Paul Nash: Article in *The Times*, May 1933, quoted in *Paul Nash as Designer* by Susan Lambert (London, Victoria and Albert Museum, 1975)

[24] Gordon Russell: 'The Work of the Royal Designers for Industry'. Lecture given to the DIA, 6 October 1948, and reprinted from *The Journal of the Royal Society of Arts*, October 1948

[25] Quoted John Blake: *The Practical Idealists* (London, Lund Humphries, 1969)

[26] Quoted Christian Barman: *The Man Who Built London Transport*, ibid.

[27] Walter Crane: Interview in *Daily News*, 20 October 1896

[28] Philip Morton Shand: 'Type Forms in Great Britain'. Article in *Die Form*, Berlin, 1930, quoted Stephen Bayley: *In Good Shape* (London, Design Council, 1979)

[29] Lewis F.Day: Article in *Art Journal*, October 1900

[30] Quoted Alison Adburgham: *Liberty's: A Biography of A Shop* (London, George Allen & Unwin, 1975)

29
Ebonised wood sideboard in esoteric style, designed by
E.W.Godwin and made by William Watt, c.1870. The
hinges and handles are silverplated and the panels are
embossed Japanese leather paper. Victoria and Albert
Museum.

The 1880s

30
Ebonised oak table, designed by E.W.Godwin and made by William Watt, c.1870. City of Bristol Museum and Art Gallery.

The 1880s was a period of extraordinary activity in the visual arts and a time at which many of the basic elements of the next hundred years' development of design in Britain are first discernible.

An idea of 'the spirit of true design' was in the air, and this implied the shedding of historic precedents, traditional superfluities, and aiming for a new style of freshness, directness and simplicity. Through this decade, the principles of functional efficiency, the fitness-for-purpose doctrines which were destined to dominate British design theory for many years to come, found their most persuasive expression in the metalwork of Christopher Dresser. E.W.Godwin's astonishing, stark, geometric furniture, made by William Watt, whose catalogue, *Art Furniture*, was published in 1877, helped to popularise the intellectual pared-down style.

At the same time, a small foretaste of the many contradictions of British design history and indeed in some ways a reflection of the paradox embodied in the dominating figure of the decade, William Morris, the mood of high ideals and austerity was balanced by a style of unprecedented richness, even fantasy, especially in textile and pottery design. The purity and reticence of much of the design of the Aesthetic Movement, obviously influenced by the art of Japan, was offset, as time went on, by the relative robustness, the self-conscious Englishness, of early Arts and Crafts design. The decade in which Dresser did much of his best work was also the decade in which Morris established his textile printing works at Merton Abbey on the Wandle; in which Walter Crane made patterns in many different media – wallpapers, textiles, ceramics, illustration – most of them entrancingly ingenious and elaborate; and William De Morgan was decorating pottery with unsurpassed exuberance and idiosyncrasy.

It was in the 1880s that the choice of special objects with which to live surrounded, one's furniture and furnishings, one's wallpapers and carpets, glass, pottery and silver, became established, in sophisticated circles, as a considerable skill, if not an art. Many handbooks of good taste were published, and believed in. Many old-established firms appeared in new aesthetic guises, calling themselves Art Furniture-makers or Art Potters. New aesthetic shops, emporiums of life-style, were set up for the assistance of the doubtful or faint-hearted, performing rather the same function as Habitat stores much later on.

Liberty's of Regent Street, founded in 1875 as an importer of Eastern merchandise, had by 1883 opened its own furnishing and decorating studios under the direction of Leonard F.Wyburd who rapidly built up a large, stylistically

31
Side table in ebonised oak, designed by E.W.Godwin and made by William Watt, c.1870. City of Bristol Museum and Art Gallery.

32
Oak writing desk, designed by A.H.Mackmurdo for the Century Guild, 1886. William Morris Gallery, Walthamstow.

33
Rush-seated chair in ebonised beech, a revival of a traditional Sussex design sold by Morris, Marshall, Faulkner & Co. from the mid-1860s onwards. This chair, in its own period, was extremely popular and it started an important ruralist tradition of chair design, British and international, Gimson to Magistretti. Wrote J.W.Mackail, Morris's first biographer: 'of all the specific minor improvements in common household objects due to Morris, the rush-bottomed Sussex chair perhaps takes the first place'.
Private collection.

coherent collection of designs in many different materials, some made in Liberty's own workshops, some made under contract by outside factories. There was even a Costume Department supervised by the avant-garde architect E.W.Godwin, and the aim was to sell goods with a consistent visual image, a kind of design package, to Liberty's aesthetically-conscious clientele. A similar exercise, an early example of corporate image-making, was well under way by the later 1870s and early 1880s not far from Liberty's, in Lower Regent Street, where Howell & James, originally metalwork specialists and general furnishers, had become the most prestigious suppliers of art pottery, claiming to be internationally known for their efforts to popularise works of high art and good taste. In those years of prosperity, art metalwork continued to be made in their own workshops, but pottery was manufactured to their specification by outside firms such as Doulton and Minton, and marked with the Howell and James stamp. Another remarkable example of

34
'Tulip' chintz designed by William Morris and originally printed by
Thomas Wardle at Leek, 1875. William Morris Gallery, Walthamstow.

35
'Cromer Bird' cretonne designed by A.H.Mackmurdo
for the Century Guild, c.1884. William Morris Gallery, Walthamstow.

36
'Wild Tulip' wallpaper designed by William Morris and
hand-printed by Jeffrey and Co., 1884. William Morris
Gallery, Walthamstow.

what was later to be known as 'design management' was the development of
W.B.Simpson, a relatively humble firm of London housepainters and decorators,
into a well-known company of art-tile painters, who commissioned a succession of
reputable artists to decorate their tiles and design tile murals (which included the
tiled refreshment room and grill room at the Victoria and Albert Museum.) Tile
blanks were supplied by commercial factories, painted, glazed and fired in Simpson's
workshops, and marked W.B.Simpson. Jeffrey & Co. of Islington printed a special
series of art wallpapers for Simpson. Some of these were designed by Lewis F.Day.

As successful as Liberty's in terms of public image was William Morris's own
company, which started in 1861 with the title Morris, Marshall, Faulkner & Co.,
Fine Art Workmen, later to become Morris & Co. The basic idea, the result of a
fruitless search by Morris and his friends for congenial furnishings for their own
houses, was to set up a 'manufactory of all things necessary for the decoration of
the house', and the founder partners included Ford Madox Brown, Dante Gabriel
Rossetti, Edward Burne-Jones and Philip Webb, the architect. In such an era of
aesthetic enterprises, the idea of a working band of brother artists (though Morris
in fact was the only really active member of the group), linked with the concept of
the moral worth of handicraft (though many of Morris's designs were, of course,
produced commercially in large quantities), had obvious attractions. The Firm, as it
was known in Morris circles, moved to premises of its own in Queen Square in
1865, and in 1877 opened a showroom in Oxford Street. By the 1880s, 'Morris' had
become a household word, as potent as Laura Ashley in the 1970s. Morris products
appealed most to the thinking middle classes, the kind of people who were moving
into Norman Shaw houses in Bedford Park, the first of the Garden Suburbs which

'The Angel with the Trumpet' cretonne designed by Herbert Horne for the Century Guild, c.1884. The initials CG are intertwined in the design which, printed mainly in browns and greens and ochres, shows the murky symbolism so peculiar to this period. William Morris Gallery, Walthamstow.

38

'Brother Rabbit' chintz by William Morris, 1883, a design incorporating Morris's favourite flora and fauna. According to May Morris, the family was reading *Uncle Remus* at Kelmscott Manor at the time. William Morris Society.

was then under construction, and soon, as Walter Crane recollected later, 'no home with any claim to decorative charm was felt to be complete without its vine and fig tree so to speak – from Queen Square'. Besides the William Morris wallpapers and textiles, the Morris Sussex chair became almost a cult object which, by the 1880s, was an established feature of the interiors of the cognoscenti: a forerunner of quantities of peasant-inspired furniture in Britain and America over the next century, a symbol of sophisticated simple life.

William Morris was an early, and unique, example of the designer entrepreneur, a man whose considerable creative impulses led him to work in the commercial world, as designer, as manufacturer, as retailer. (The fact that, as a socialist, he much despised general commercial practice makes his achievement all the more extraordinary.) It was obviously a time of great artistic optimism. In the early 1880s, Christopher Dresser, the most original designer of the day, was involved in multifarious commercial ventures: an oriental import firm, Dresser and Holme; an aesthetic shop in Bond Street, the Art Furnishers' Alliance, which was formed 'for

39
'Poppy' dessert doily in silk and linen damask, one of a
set entitled 'Flora's Retinue' designed by Walter Crane,
1893. William Morris Gallery, Walthamstow.

40
'Single Flower' cretonne designed by A.H.Mackmurdo
for the Century Guild, c.1882. On account of
Mackmurdo's swirling foliage, this design makes an
almost statutory appearance in books on the origins of
art nouveau. William Morris Gallery, Walthamstow.

the purpose of supplying all kinds of artistic house-furnishing material, including furniture, carpets, wall-decorations, hangings, pottery, table glass, silversmiths' wares, hardware, and whatever is necessary to our household selection'. Every item for sale was subject to approval by the art director, Dr Dresser, who, at this same period was acting as designer, on a freelance basis, to Hukin & Heath and James Dixon, manufacturers of metalwork, and Linthorpe Pottery. Though not all Dresser's enterprises were successful, the Art Furnishers' Alliance going into liquidation in 1883, the sheer range of his design-work is impressive: cast iron, silver, pottery, glass, woodwork, textiles for at least a dozen factories. He was also writing some influential books, among them *Japan*, published in 1882.

It is possible to see the 1880s as the period of origin for the design profession, although the designer of those days would be entitled 'art adviser' or 'art superintendent'. But his role was beginning to be defined. Its commercial importance was beginning to be recognised. Walter Crane, painter, printmaker and illustrator, was, for instance, also greatly in demand as a designer for wallpapers and fabrics, printed, woven and embroidered, for pottery and tiles. Like Morris, Walter Crane had become a name to conjure with. As Mark Girouard points out in *Sweetness and Light: The Queen Anne Movement*, a Walter Crane frieze in the drawing room, Crane tiles and wallpapers throughout the house and even Walter Crane picture books in the nursery, had become *de rigueur* in many of the fashionable houses of the period, and in 1880 Crane was appointed Art Superintendent of the London Decorating Company. Another famous professional designer, Lewis F.Day, a formidable precursor of the twentieth-century design consultant, had set up his own office in London in 1870, branching out from his first speciality, stained glass, to design for the wallpaper and textile industries as well as pottery, furniture and glass. He became art director of Turnbull & Stockdale, the textile manufacturers, in 1881. In the 1880s and 1890s, especially through his widely distributed wallpapers and textiles – designs as evocative of their period as those of Claud Lovat Fraser in the 1920s, Lucienne Day in the 1950s – he had a very direct influence on public taste. In 1884, another very early example of commercial freelance design studio was opened by Arthur Silver. The Silver Studio, which sold designs successfully on the Continent as well as in Britain, was professional in outlook rather than pioneering, bringing good design to the bourgeoisie. It lasted until 1963.

The dawning art consciousness of industry showed itself in many forms in the late nineteenth century, the most immediately significant of which was the highly popular Art Pottery movement. Remnants of this are still around us. Art Pottery, of course, was very much a feature of the Aesthetic period. In the early 1870s, Henry Doulton of Doulton of Lambeth, the mainstay of whose production then consisted of stoneware drain-pipes and conduits, had yielded to persuasion from John Sparkes, head of the School of Art at Lambeth, for a number of students from the school, under Sparkes' supervision, to decorate experimental ranges of Doulton's salt-glazed stoneware. This policy continued and developed and by the 1880s Doulton's studio was employing over 200 artists, male and female. At almost the same time, Minton had opened Art Pottery Studios in South Kensington. The biscuit pottery was brought from Minton's factory in Stoke-on-Trent for decoration and impression with the mark 'Minton's Art Pottery Studio, Kensington Gore'. In

41
Copper and brass kettle designed by Christopher Dresser and made by Benham & Froud, c.1885. Victoria and Albert Museum.

42
Stand for 6 eggs, electroplate, designed by Christopher Dresser and made by Hukin & Heath, c.1878. Victoria and Albert Museum.

43
Teapot, electroplate, with ebony finial and handle, designed by Christopher Dresser and made by Hukin & Heath, 1878. Robertson collection at the Royal Pavilion, Art Gallery and Museums, Brighton.

44
Folding toast-rack, electroplate, designed by Christopher Dresser and made by Hukin & Heath, 1881. Robertson collection at the Royal Pavilion, Art Gallery and Museums, Brighton.

45
Ebony-handled teapot from electroplate tea service designed by Christopher Dresser for James Dixon, 1880. Dresser was designing regularly for this Sheffield firm in the early 1880s and their contemporary catalogue illustrates dozens of designs of an extreme stylistic non-conformity. Victoria and Albert Museum.

46
Tall jug and beakers in salt-glazed stoneware, made by
the Martin Brothers, c.1893. The three potter brothers,
who set up their joint studio in Southall in 1877, are best
known for their grotesque birds, modelled by Wallace
Martin. But they were prolific potters, and their more
classic pieces are interesting too. Victoria and Albert
Museum.

60

the late 1870s, Wilcock and Company, a Leeds manufacturer of drain-pipes and firebricks, had introduced a new kind of art pottery, Burmantofts Faïence, which was sold by Howell & James in Lower Regent Street. Through the 1880s, there were many more art potteries to come. This same pattern of the large industrial firm supporting, and in ideal cases being stimulated by, an experimental craft studio was developed with particular conviction in Scandinavia from the 1920s onwards.

As well as such commercially-sponsored art potteries, there was a growing number of independent, individualistic potters. This was really the first sign of the modern studio-pottery movement which was to dominate the coming century of British craft activity. In Devon, in the 1880s, C.H.Brannam, a potter who had been to School of Art in Barnstaple, had begun producing the well-known and peculiarly artistic 'Barum Ware', for which Liberty's became the agents. At this period, too, the Martin Brothers were at work in Southall, producing their very distinctive, often startlingly eccentric pottery designs in salt-glazed stoneware. At Clevedon Court, near Bath, Sir Edmund Elton was experimenting, from 1880, with shapes and glazes many of which were extraordinarily innovative. (He once said of himself, rather endearingly, that 'if an ignorant country baronet set to work to make mud-pies and didn't know anything about it, and used plenty of glazing he was bound to turn out something queer'.) From 1882, William De Morgan was installed at Merton Abbey, having erected his own buildings and kilns beside the disused print works which William Morris had converted for the manufacture of his chintzes. Though De Morgan's pottery shows a multitude of influences, Spanish, Italian, Persian, as well as contemporary English-Aesthetic, its decorative qualities are thoroughly original. De Morgan was almost obsessively involved in workshop experiments, in technical development, a bias typical of advanced artistic thinking in this first great era of fine art workmanship.

Technique was to become one of the very central interests, a kind of watchword of the times, as the decade progressed and the preoccupations of the Aesthetic Movement gradually gave way to the ideals of Arts and Crafts. William Morris's theories of truth to material, the idea that designers should work to get the most from their material 'in such a way as honours it most', began to come into general artistic currency, together with the principle, to be developed greatly by later design theorists, that not only should it be altogether obvious to the beholder what that material is, but that the material should have received some special treatment which served to exploit its intrinsic qualities: as Morris maintained, something should have been done with it which is specially natural to it, something that could not be done with any other. William Morris was a toweringly influential figure in the artistic circles of the time, referred to reverentially as 'the Master Craftsman', and it was generally acknowledged that his example stimulated the very widespread interest and activity through the 1880s and 1890s not only in the central craft areas, in weaving, in woodwork, in metalwork, in pottery, but also in the more esoteric crafts, from the revival of embroidery and bookbinding to stained glass and plasterwork, inlay and intarsia, gesso and sgraffito.

The late Victorian individual workshop movement, in some ways very similar in spirit to the workshop movement of the 1970s, was of course a protest movement, a movement of revulsion against prevailing taste and current manufacturing practice. It was in a way rather amateur in concept. Morris, Marshall, Faulkner & Co. was founded in a spirit of camaraderie, a group of friends of the same outlook who liked the idea – in the early years at least – of co-operative working. The Century Guild, founded in 1882 by A.H.Mackmurdo, architect and self-taught craftsman, a disciple of Ruskin's, had similarly wide-ranging aims, the intention to 'restore building, decoration, glass painting, pottery, wood-carving and metal to their rightful place beside painting and sculpture', and a comparably loose and rather dilettante structure. Again, it was a gathering of more or less like-minded artists and designers, among them Selwyn Image, Herbert Horne and Clement Heaton. William De Morgan, Heywood Sumner and C.F.A.Voysey were, also, from time to time, working with the Guild, which, typically in an age of the all-round designer, an age in which William Morris composed epics while weaving tapestries, produced its own quarterly magazine, *The Hobby Horse*. Some of the work, especially the textiles and the furniture designed by Mackmurdo himself, is peculiarly innovative, strangely blending Japanese and English eighteenth-century influences. But the Guild itself in the end came to very little and in 1888 it was disbanded.

That same year, as the Century Guild dwindled away, another Guild, the Guild of Handicraft, was started. This was to be a larger, more ambitious venture, the pattern of the other Guilds to come. It was set up in the East End of London by a young architect-idealist, C.R.Ashbee, whose aim was not just to improve aesthetic standards, to make buildings and the objects which went into them more beautiful, but also, more importantly, to improve the standards of life of the workmen, the producers. The Guild of Handicraft, founded on the Ruskin tenets of joy in handicraft, of man's innate creative instinct, had a solemn moral purpose. It was educational, with a School of Handicraft working alongside it, and a full programme of cultural activities planned to enlarge the horizons of the craftsmen. Its reputation and influence grew quickly and its repertoire of crafts expanded from base metalwork, furniture, interior decorating, modelling to wrought ironwork and the wonderfully original silver and jewellery for which C.R.Ashbee is now so widely known.

By the end of the 1880s, the moral issues of art and craftsmanship seemed almost to be outweighing the aesthetic ones: the relation of the fine artist and the craftsman; the relation of the handicrafts to machine production; the whole wide role of the artist-craftsman in society. These were all subjects under long discussion at the earnest, convivial and, needless to say, male-dominated meetings which were so much a feature of this period. Gatherings of the Art Workers' Guild, founded in 1884, and including in its membership almost all the leading artist-craftsmen (and craftsmen-artists) of the day; meetings of the Arts and Crafts Exhibition Society, formed in 1888 with Walter Crane as President declaiming confidently that 'the true root and basis of all Art lies in the handicrafts'. A constant theme in the writings and speeches of these groups, the membership of which in fact was fairly interchangeable, was that of the importance of the personal element in art, a claim for the rightful recognition of the individual designer. This idea of individual artistic responsibility, a strongly moral concept, also turned out to have considerable commercial advantages in that it identified particular designers, giving them a public image, a glamour and a kudos. The 'personal element' was to develop greatly in the full-blown Arts and Crafts movement of the next two decades.

48
Inlaid oak chest designed in the late 1890s by Ernest
Barnsley. Although rarer than that of his younger
brother Sidney, for he spent most of his life in
architectural practice, Ernest Barnsley's furniture has
much of the same quality and character: a similar love of
straightforward, sound construction; a comparable
fascination with countrified traditions, as exemplified in
the domed lid and inlaid chevrons of this masterly piece
of Arts and Crafts design. Leicestershire Museums.

The 1890s and early 1900s

The Arts and Crafts movement dominates the period from 1890 to 1910, two decades of almost bewildering richness, both in terms of individual creative energy and also sheer range of design activity. It was a period of marvellous inventiveness and confidence, during which British prestige abroad was at its height.

The visual style stretched from the extremely plain and simple, the box-like construction of the pseudo-peasant furniture joked about so much by its detractors, to the highly ornate, associative and symbolic Arts and Crafts artefacts, especially the metalwork. From the basic rural idiom so popular in Europe – exemplified by the clarity and sweetness, the perfectly-judged prettiness of C.F.A.Voysey's designs for wallpapers and textiles – it ascends to the very urbane sophistication of much of the metalwork designed by C.R.Ashbee, the high-flown fantasies of Henry Wilson's silver. It was in some (though not in all) ways a hugely tolerant, imaginative period in British design history. And if in the end, as the nationalistic forces of *Jugendstil* spread over Europe, the Arts and Crafts in Britain tended to recede into a rather sentimental Celtic-inspired quaintness, this should not be allowed to obliterate the quality and force of the movement in its early years nor to belittle the considerable influence of Arts and Crafts on what came later.

Design at this time of course was deeply rooted in the architectural movement of the day. Architecture was regarded in progressive design circles as the 'mother Art', the centre of activity, and it is significant that most of the successful designers of the period had had an architectural training. William Morris himself, acknowledged by so many of the younger architect-designers as their prophet and their mentor, had worked with G.E.Street, and although he did not afterwards practise as an architect, his view of design was always architecture-orientated. His friend and contemporary, Philip Webb, who was also much respected by the younger generation and who must be held at least partly responsible for the cult of the commonplace in Arts and Crafts, was an architect obsessively concerned with detail. His belief that the architect should control totally all aspects of a building, structural and decorative, practical and spiritual, had immense and obvious influence on the philosophy and practice of such Art Workers' Guild architects as W.R.Lethaby, Ernest Gimson, E.G.Prior. This idea of design totality, coherence of all visual aspects of a building, can be seen in the work of many Scottish architect-designers of the period, sometimes sublimely so in C.R.Mackintosh's buildings. Another especially interesting example is the work of Frank Brangwyn, the painter and designer, whose decorative schemes, though few survive intact, seem to have been *tours de*

49
Oak dresser, c.1898, a design of typical assurance by
C.F.A.Voysey, in a naïve style of extreme sophistication.
The elongated uprights, the brass hinges and escutcheons,
give it a visual character almost, but not quite, quaint.
Royal Pavilion, Art Gallery and Museums, Brighton.

force of Arts and Crafts perfectionism, with as much attention lavished on the patterns for the ashtrays as on the designs for the furniture and murals.

The craft experiments, the fascination with techniques, which had been so characteristic a feature of the 1880s, continued unabated through the 1890s. *The Studio*, founded in 1893, almost a house magazine for Arts and Crafts, carried detailed reports of these developments. In its first issues, for instance, it included 'Notes on Gesso Work' by Walter Crane, a commentary on T.J.Cobden-Sanderson's new bookbinding, and a feature on the progress of Alexander Fisher's early attempts at mastering enamelling (described as 'a very arduous undertaking, being more the work of a chemist than an artist'). It was still the age of individual artist-craftsmen, enthusiasts, inventors, almost showmen. In his old age, William Morris, inveterate experimenter, focused his attention on the revival of hand printing

50
Wash-stand in oak, with block-printed curtain, designed c.1895. This is the first known piece of furniture by Ambrose Heal, in the basic cottage style he was later to make famous, an idiom so unpopular with Heal's employees they tended to refer to it as 'prison furniture'. Heal collection, Heal and Son.

51
Domino table and barrel-shaped chairs in oak with
brown stain finish, designed by Charles Rennie
Mackintosh for the Argyle Street Tea-Rooms, 1897. The
top surface was for playing dominoes, then a very
popular Glasgow pastime; the lower shelves were meant
to hold the coffee cups and the unspent dominoes of four
players. The design proved so functionally successful
that it was revived for the Ingram Street Tea-Rooms
fourteen years later. Mackintosh collection, Glasgow
School of Art.

52
Macassar ebony cabinet on stand, inlaid with mother-of-pearl, designed by Ernest Gimson, c.1907. Gimson's reputation for unsurpassing honesty, well deserved as it was, tends to obliterate his love of decoration; his penchant for the courtly; the elaborate and urbane style of much of his production. This cabinet shows Gimson at his most ornate and formal; yet somehow it avoids all sense of blandness or pomposity. It has a kind of innocence, self-confidence and sweetness which makes it one of the great classics of its period. Leicestershire Museums.

and in 1890 set up the Kelmscott Press in Hammersmith. In 1894, Harold Rathbone had established the Della Robbia Pottery in Birkenhead, and four years later, W. Howson Taylor founded the Ruskin Pottery in Smethwick, producing a whole range of experimental glazes. The individual innovative urge was very strong in many design areas in the 1890s. But gradually, alongside these triumphs of technique, a new preoccupation began to spread infectiously, a new interest not just in the work but in the workshop, in life as well as craft, in the idea of communities of working craftsmen. When in 1890 the Birmingham Guild of Handicraft was founded, on the model of C.R. Ashbee's Guild in London, one of its main concerns was the well-being of the workmen, a well-being which, it was felt by the founders, conscientious citizens who had read their Ruskin, was likely to result from civilised conditions of working life, especially the pleasure gained from making things by hand.

53
Ladderback chair in ash with rush seat, adapted by
Ernest Gimson from a traditional country design, late
19th century. Inspired by Philip Clissett, the
Herefordshire chair bodger who supplied chairs to
the Art Workers' Guild in London, Ernest Gimson
himself learned the basic skills of chair-making and
designed a number of variations of the turned wood
country chair, which soon became the standard seating
of the Arts and Crafts movement. This particular chair,
with its unusually decorative back, was used by the
bookbinder Katharine Adams at her bindery in
Broadway. Mr and Mrs Michael Rossiter.

54
Lattice-backed oak settee with cushion seat by Sidney Barnsley, c.1919. A handsome (though hardly comfortable) piece of furniture made for the sculptor and carver William Simmonds in simplest Barnsley style, with subtle detailing. Cheltenham Art Gallery and Museum.

The love of rural life which has had such a strong impact, for better or for worse, on twentieth-century design development, is easy to trace back to the idealists of this period, the back-to-the-land craftsmen and the simple-life protagonists. In 1893, three years after the formation of Kenton & Co., experimental furniture workshops in London in which they had both been founder-partners, Ernest Gimson and Sidney Barnsley travelled out to the Cotswolds to set up their own craft workshops, where they were joined by Sidney's brother, Ernest. Both in terms of the visual style which they established, and in terms of their whole approach to art and workmanship, Gimson and the Barnsleys have had an influence above and beyond their own small individual output. In 1896, with a comparable instinct to revivify the rural traditions, similarly inspired by a congenial country setting, Godfrey Blount was to establish the Haslemere Peasant Industries, promoting weaving, embroidery, simple furniture and other country crafts and forming an associated Peasant Arts Society. It was Haslemere too, then something of a centre for small handweaving workshops, which Edmund Hunter, who was later to become a well-known designer in the textiles industry, chose as the ideal site for his own enterprise, St Edmundsbury Weaving Works, in 1901. The following year, a venture which even in that era of artistic optimism seems astonishingly romantic and ambitious, C.R.Ashbee and the craftsmen of the Guild of Handicraft, their wives and children, in all 150 people, moved out from the East End of London to start

55
Oak wardrobe with stained wood panels, from the
Liberty 'Athelstan' range, probably designed by
Leonard F.Wyburd and made in Liberty's workshops,
c.1903. Around this period, era of the *faux naïve*,
Liberty's was promoting successfully a species of outsize
nursery furniture: for instance this giant wardrobe, with
its picture-book panels and cut-out heart motifs. Royal
Pavilion, Art Gallery and Museums, Brighton.

working in the peaceful rural setting of Chipping Campden, Gloucestershire. Ashbee
hoped he would improve both his craftsmen and their craftsmanship by bringing
them in touch with 'the elemental things of life'.

Considering the widespread concern with handicrafts among the more progressive
designers and design theorists of the time, it was perfectly predictable that when the
LCC, through its Technical Education Board, decided to open a new school, the
Central School, in London, this should turn out to be a school of craftsmanship.
Up to then the design courses in the colleges of art, the Royal College of Art in
London and the provincial colleges, had concentrated on two-dimensional design,
on pattern-making, and in fact they had specialised in training teachers. But the
Central School, which opened in 1896, was altogether different, a new species of art
school. The co-Principal, to start with, was W.R.Lethaby, architect, designer and
by then a leading figure in Art Workers' Guild circles, a respected spokesman for
Arts and Crafts principles. He managed to gather around him a teaching staff
which, from the first, included many of the most distinguished craftsmen and
designers, such Arts and Crafts practitioners as Halsey Ricardo, the architect;
Douglas Cockerell, the bookbinder; R.Catterson Smith, who taught wallpaper and

textile design; Edward Johnston who taught lettering and illuminating and whose department was soon to be developed to cover book design and printing. (His students included Eric Gill, Noel Rooke and Graily Hewitt.) The success of the Central School, which very quickly established itself as the most progressive and best-organised school of design in Europe, must mainly be attributed to Lethaby's own gentle powers of leadership, his total conviction, expressed in his most famous essay 'Art and Workmanship', that 'a work of art is first of all a well-made thing'. In 1900 Lethaby also became the first Professor of Design at the Royal College of Art, holding both appointments simultaneously in the period up to World War I. He was in a position of extraordinary influence on the new generation of designers, and his ideas of the importance of handcraftsmanship as the basis of designing, the essential element in the training of designers, helped to shape the design education of the time. These views affected education on the Continent, especially in Germany: they are obvious in the workshop structure of the early Bauhaus. They were still in force in art colleges in Britain, including the Royal College of Art, until well into the 1950s.

Although the Arts and Crafts movement seems clear-cut in its theories, acknowledging its debt to Ruskin and Morris, it interpreted these principles, as Morris did himself, with some sophistication. In practice, Arts and Crafts were a great deal less dogmatic than might have been imagined. Except by the most doctrinaire of fine-art workmen, the crafts were not seen as an end in themselves.

56
Armchair in walnut, inlaid with mother-of-pearl, designed by George Walton and made for Liberty & Co. by William Birch, c.1899. Victoria and Albert Museum.
57
Ebonised dining chair with cane seat and back, designed by George Walton, c.1903. Victoria and Albert Museum.
58
Three-sided oak cupboard with brass handles, designed by Ernest Gimson, c.1906. Leicestershire Museums.

59
Waitresses' chair in oak with black stain finish, designed by Charles Rennie Mackintosh for Miss Cranston's Tea-Rooms, c.1904. Mackintosh collection, Glasgow School of Art.
60
Semicircular oak settle with black stain finish, designed by Charles Rennie Mackintosh for the Willow Tea-Rooms, 1904. Mackintosh collection, Glasgow School of Art.

They were regarded as more of a potential force for the good of society at large. The idea of interaction of hand and machine, the role of the craftsman as the humanising factor, the controller of standard, in industrial production, was becoming a popular tenet of this period and a recurring theme in the deliberations of the National Association for the Advancement of Art and its Application to Industry, a society founded in 1887, whose members included leading Arts and Crafts designers. Through the 1890s, a number of designers whose origins and loyalties lay with the Arts and Crafts movement were to be seen designing for machine production with no apparent self-consciousness or anguish. W.A.S.Benson, for instance, an associate of Morris and a founder of the Art Workers' Guild, built up a highly mechanised small factory in Hammersmith to produce his metal lamps, vases, dishes and so on in considerable quantity. ('He preferred', said his *Times* obituary, 'to approach his subject as an engineer rather than a hand-worker; to produce beautiful forms by machinery on a commercial scale rather than single works of art'). From 1895, C.F.A.Voysey was working prolifically as a designer for James Morton of Alexander Morton & Co., the textile firm, establishing a pattern of close co-operation over a

61
Smoker's cabinet, oak with dark stain finish, designed by Charles Rennie Mackintosh, with repoussé copper panels by his wife, Margaret Macdonald, c.1900. This cabinet, which was shown at the Secessionist Exhibition in Vienna, was, in its very idiosyncratic character, with its touches of eroticism, the antithesis of mainstream English Arts and Crafts, much closer in feeling to the Expressionist design tradition which developed on the Continent. Mackintosh collection, Glasgow School of Art.

62
Oak armchair with inlaid decoration, designed by
E.G.Punnett, made by William Birch, 1901. This chair,
manufactured in High Wycombe, is one of many
interesting examples of the way in which Arts and Crafts
ideas about design – forthrightness of structure, fitness
of decoration – percolated through to commercial
production. Victoria and Albert Museum.

63
'Purple Bird', silk and wool double cloth, designed by
C.F.A.Voysey for Alexander Morton, c.1899.
Manchester College of Art collection, The Whitworth
Art Gallery, University of Manchester.

long period between enlightened patron and his 'art adviser', an important element
in twentieth-century British design history.

By 1896, *The Studio* was commenting: 'Now a "Voysey wallpaper" sounds almost
as familiar as "Morris Chintz" or a "Liberty Silk".' The cult of personal style, the
singling out of special objects, the trick of recognising individual designers: all these
tendencies, clearly discernible in the 1880s, became even more pronounced by
the later 1890s. The prime experts in house style, Liberty & Co., extended their
successful policy, marketing their famous range of pseudo-Saxon furniture, designed
in their own Studio, as well as commissioning furniture from well-known freelance
designers, such as Voysey and George Walton. From 1899, they developed 'Cymric'
silverware and 'Tudric' pewter, designed in craftsman's style by professional
designers, Archibald Knox and Rex Silver in particular, and mostly made for
Liberty's by Haseler's in Birmingham. They also added to their reputation as
leading dealers in art pottery by introducing Moorcroft's 'Florian' collection, as

64
Coffee-pot, hot milk jug and cream jug, electroplate, probably designed by Arthur Dixon, made by the Birmingham Guild of Handicraft (motto: 'By Hammer and Hand') between 1902 and 1908. Private collection.

65
Silver sugar bowl with double handles, each set with a green chrysoprase, designed by C.R.Ashbee, made by the Guild of Handicraft, 1902. The long, thin, looping handles are typical of Ashbee, often used in his silverware, to great effect. The Worshipful Company of Goldsmiths.

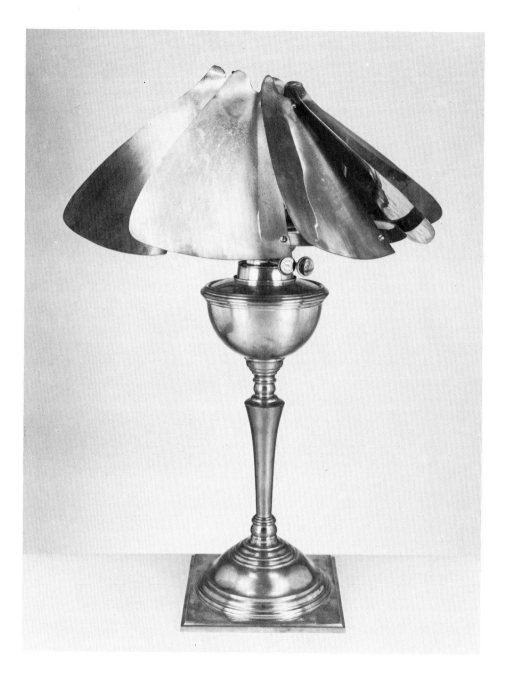

66
Brass lamp designed by W.A.S.Benson, c.1895, and
manufactured in the small-scale factory which Benson,
an important link between the Arts and Crafts and mass
production, set up in Hammersmith in the early 1880s.
Victoria and Albert Museum.

well as rural pottery from Farnham (listed in Liberty's contemporary catalogues as
'Green Ware'), and the range of garden pots made especially for Liberty's at the art
pottery at Compton, Guildford, Surrey, founded and run by Mary Watts, wife of
G.F.Watts, the famous painter.

67
Silver christening mug designed by C.R.Ashbee for his
daughter, Felicity, 1913. The mug, with its 'Wise Old
Owl' quotation, shows the Arts and Crafts delight in
decorative inscription, a tradition handed on to Eric Gill
and his adherents. Felicity Ashbee.

68
Silver carriage clock with enamelled face, made for
Liberty & Co., 1900. The wry inscription, 'TEMPUS
FUGIT', is a characteristic Arts and Crafts device. On
loan to City of Bristol Museum and Art Gallery.

Heal style, in direct competition to 'Stile Liberty', first got underway in 1898,
when the first catalogue of furniture designs by Ambrose Heal, a range of bedroom
furniture in oak, was circulated. The family firm of Heal in Tottenham Court Road
was already well-established as a manufacturer of bedding and supplier of
traditional furniture. Ambrose Heal, a member of the new generation (like Geoffrey
Dunn of Dunn's of Bromley in the 1930s) pursued the more progressive design
thinking of his time. He trained with a cabinet-maker, and this workshop experience
influenced his designs for furniture which, compared with the fanciful urbanities of
Liberty's, were more consciously countrified, designed for plainer living: the
commercial consequence of Arts and Crafts. In 1900, a Heal bedroom was assembled

69
Firedogs in brass and steel, designed by Ernest Gimson
and probably made by Alfred Bucknell, foreman of
Gimson's smithy at Sapperton, c.1905. The pierced
decoration based on the carnation, with its strong
associations of sweet summers, English gardens, is true
to the feeling of ruralist nostalgia in the Arts and Crafts
movement. Leicestershire Museums.

70
Cutlery, electroplate, designed by Charles Rennie
Mackintosh for the Ingram Street Tea-Rooms, 1903.
Glasgow Museums and Art Galleries.
71
Cutlery, electroplate, designed by C.F.A.Voysey and
made by C.W.Fletcher, Sheffield, c.1902.
Mrs J.Wellington.
72
Silver cutlery, designed by George Walton and made by
W.Comyns, 1902–3. Victoria and Albert Museum.
73
'Dewdrop' finger-bowl and tumbler, made for Liberty &
Co., c.1902. Victoria and Albert Museum.
74
Casket, silverplate and copper with cedarwood lining,
made by the Birmingham Guild of Handicraft, early
20th century. Private collection.
75
One of a pair of brass candle-sconces, designed by
Ernest Gimson and made by Alfred Bucknell, c.1907.
Cheltenham Art Gallery and Museum.

for the Paris Exhibition. The furniture, in oak inlaid with figured ebony and pewter, was designed by Ambrose Heal: the setting was by his cousin Cecil Brewer, the architect (later co-founder of the DIA). The room-set shows remarkable attention to detail, down to tapestry bed-hangings by Godfrey Blount of Haslemere Peasant Industries, and the *Architectural Review* commented: 'It almost goes without saying that the materials have been very carefully selected, and the work, which has been carried out under Mr Heal's personal supervision, is a triumph of craftmanship'.

In fact, as it developed, Heal's plain oak furniture was perhaps not so much a triumph of craftsmanship (though standards of craftsmanship were never less than decent) as it was a triumph for commercial acumen. The market at that time was absolutely ready for it. The British middle classes have always had a craving for a somewhat spurious peasant style of living – a tradition one can follow through from

76
Silver casket set with opal matrix, designed by Archibald Knox for Liberty & Co., 1903, in the quasi-Celtic idiom so popular in turn-of-the-century art metalwork. Victoria and Albert Museum.

Heal in 1900 to Habitat much later. This was a form of furnishing especially in fashion in the Edwardian era in the new high-minded homesteads of the Garden Cities and the Garden Suburbs around London, and just as the denizens of Bedford Park had welcomed William Morris wallpapers and fabrics and rush-seated country chairs, so now the prospective residents of Letchworth were eager for the reasonably-priced oak of Ambrose Heal: the dressers and the bookcases, the wheelback dining chairs, the china racks, the coal scuttles, the Cottage Table Wares. Before long, Heal acquired a great many imitators, most of them less sensitive to visual consistency, and the catalogues of furnishing shops throughout the country, from Glasgow to Bristol, began promoting furniture which was a curious hybrid of English country style and Continental *art nouveau*.

In the end, needless to say, this did the Arts and Crafts no good. In the face of

77
Large double-handled jar by Della Robbia Pottery, late 19th century. This design, with its rich green and yellow decoration, shows the admirably courageous fusion of Italian Renaissance style with English Arts and Crafts. Victoria and Albert Museum.

such proliferation of Arts-and-Crafts-style products, the individuality was gone, the idea meaningless. The Arts and Crafts had lost their purity and mystery. The Arts and Crafts, in fact, had become a bit banal. William Morris had died in 1896; the movement had lost its impetus and focus. It was generally obvious that Arts and Crafts Exhibition Society shows in 1903 and 1906 were less convincing than the exhibitions of the previous decade; and later exhibitions were felt to be still worse. Commercial competition, the cynical development of factory production imitating craftwork, was undermining the more conscientious workshops, upholders of the Arts and Crafts hammer-and-hand values. This, at a time of general trade depression, was certainly a factor in the final liquidation of Ashbee's Guild of Handicraft, a *débacle* which did nothing to restore the confidence of Ashbee's brother art workers. By the end of the decade it was becoming clear that the time was coming for some form of realignment. It began to be seen as the duty of designers to get out of the workshops and into the factories, an idea which became a principle and a fixation, indeed a sort of war-cry, in the naïve optimism of the period ahead.

The 1910s and 1920s

This was the period in which the concept of design for industry began to be important. In the years surrounding World War I, and even, surprisingly, while that War was raging, one can watch the evolution from Arts and Crafts ideas to a kind of a crusade to improve the standards of design for mass production, led by the Design and Industries Association. The philosophy of 'decent design for ordinary people', which the DIA propounded with such earnestness, was the dominant principle of these two decades, and indeed was still adhered to in the government efforts to influence design in British industry after World War II. But an interesting facet of this period, a development largely ignored by historians, who find it convenient to trace progress neatly from Arts and Crafts to DIA to modernism, was the resurgence, as the 1920s progressed, of an immense amount of craft activity. This was less of a formalised craft movement, more of a spontaneous springing-up of individual workshops, and the interrelation between craft and industry, hand and machine production, give this peculiarly fascinating period a character and influence very much its own.

The feeling of the time is very even, very gentle. Compared with the stylistic idiosyncrasies of Arts and Crafts design, the recurring images of DIA design are altogether steady and predictable. The Heal's weathered oak sideboards, the Dryad cane chairs, the early morning tea-sets by Carter, Stabler, Adams: such perennial favourites of the design cognoscenti of the period have an understated homeliness, a pleasant kind of primness, very much related to the (DIA-approved) reconstituted Georgian buildings of the era. This overall consistency and reticence of style makes the many sudden bursts of the exotic and the quirky all the more endearing and astonishing: the impractical Expressionism of the Omega Workshops, set up by Roger Fry and his group of artist friends, antidote to all the DIA good sense and soundness; the 'potterie sauvage' designed for Poole by Truda Carter; the dazzlingly inventive Foxton textiles of the 1920s designed by such professionals as F.Gregory Brown, Minnie McLeish and (before his early death) Claud Lovat Fraser, illustrator and stage designer, whose attraction to the fairground and the chap-book, puppet shows and pantomimes, the popular theatrical tradition, with its emphasis on colour and humour and directness, also had its influence on the contemporary scene.

The Design and Industries Association was founded formally in 1915. It was a pressure group modelled, broadly speaking, on the Deutscher Werkbund, and it introduced itself, in its first propaganda leaflet, as *A New Body with New Aims*. In a

78
Polished deal cupboard chest with black edges, designed by Ambrose Heal, c.1918. This design, a standard Heal's product included in the Cottage Furniture Catalogue, exemplifies the principles of unobtrusive decency propounded by the Design and Industries Association, of which Ambrose Heal had been a founder. Heal collection, Heal and Son.

79
Tallboy chest in English oak with laburnum handles, designed by Gordon Russell, c.1926. Up to the mid-1920s, Gordon Russell's furniture was strongly Arts and Crafts in character, obviously influenced by Gimson and Sidney Barnsley. Compared with the (slightly earlier) Heal's cupboard, no. 78, this is very much a craftsman's piece of furniture, beautiful but, in a sense, by then a little antiquated. Museum collection, Gordon Russell.

sense one should see it less as a totally new departure than a logical development, a realigment; for many of its members, including such important early committee members as Harold Stabler, Ernest Jackson, Ambrose Heal and Cecil Brewer, had been leading figures in the Arts and Crafts societies. W.R.Lethaby, a member of the Council and the *eminence grise* of the Association, was very much attuned to the precepts and the attitudes of Philip Webb and William Morris. Many of the theories of the DIA, such doctrines as the right use of materials, the proper place for ornament, the beauty of the commonplace, were all close to the most basic principles of Arts and Crafts; and almost all its aims, its belief in the national importance of improved design standards in factory production, had been under discussion for many years before. But what was new about the DIA was its insistence on the need

80
Boot cupboard in Honduras mahogany, designed by
Gordon Russell, 1925. The change in style from the Arts
and Crafts tallboy chest of the same period, no. 79,
is remarkable: instead of the old frame-and-panel
construction, the cupboard has flush fronts; the doors
are veneered blockboard; the piece has a pared-down,
completely functional appearance; and this was the
idiom which Gordon Russell, over the next few years,
successfully pursued. Museum collection, Gordon
Russell.

for urgent action and the way it was able, early on in wartime, by pointing out the
comparable excellence of German industrial products, to enlist government interest
and support. In 1915, the Board of Trade had organised an exhibition at Goldsmiths'
Hall in London under the convincing title 'Exhibition of German and Austrian
articles typifying successful design'. The accompanying leaflet, which praised
co-operation between German manufacturers and designers and the resulting
'appropriateness, technical perfection and honest workmanship' of German
products, gave the DIA a great initial impetus in its campaign for British 'Efficiency
Style'.

Lethaby, the most inspiring theorist of his period, saw it as the DIA's function to
impose some sort of visual order and serenity on a world which had become, as he

81
Oak chair with leather seat, designed by Gordon Russell, 1924. Museum collection, Gordon Russell.
82
Trolley made by the Dryad Cane Furniture Works, c.1915. Mr and Mrs S.H.Nichols.

83
Oak dining chair with bun feet and latticed back, designed by Ambrose Heal and made by Heal's from c.1926. Heal collection, Heal and Son.

saw it, a pawnshop 'full of old junk'. This urge to tidy up the visual scene, to rationalise, to simplify, was deeply sympathetic to the design-conscious industrialists and businessmen, mostly of a younger generation than Lethaby's, who joined the DIA in its early years. Of these the best known and in some ways most remarkable was Frank Pick, then a rising manager with London Underground and later Chief Executive of the London Passenger Transport Board. He was DIA Chairman from 1921. By then, with a typical solemnity and thoroughness, he had developed his own design convictions, the principles of fitness for use which he reiterated with a passionate belief. Frank Pick's work for the Underground and then for London Transport, the posters he commissioned, the classic Sans Serif typeface designed by Edward Johnston (dating back to 1916), the long collaboration with the architect Charles Holden on the underground stations and headquarters offices, the calling in of specialist designers for such details as ticket machines, directional signs, litter bins and wall-tiles, moquettes for the seat covers of LPTB vehicles: all this was an advertisement of the DIA principles on an enormous scale. It was also an early and enviable example of the science of design management in action, a justification for corporate identity before that much-overworked term had been invented. Most of all, perhaps, it has to be seen as the expression of one man's sense of vision, Pick's own sense that visual rightness was the moral thing to strive for: for these, in their own way, were still idealistic years.

The spirit of that time, its fervour and gregariousness, its dogged sense of mission, is very well recorded by Noel Carrington in *Industrial Design in Britain*. It is also referred to by Sir Gordon Russell in his autobiography, *Designer's Trade*, in which he describes his DIA induction in the early 1920s when, as a young man, he was just beginning to make furniture in Broadway, on a very tiny scale. 'I had come across

84
Cane chair, c.1910, made by Dryad, the cane works established by Harry Peach in Leicester in 1907. Though Dryad acknowledged its debt to the cane furniture then being produced in Austria and Germany, the designs arrived at through the collaboration of Peach and his friend B.J.Fletcher (head of Leicester College of Art, co-founder of the DIA) emerged as unmistakably English, British design classics. All the more unfortunate that, because of the nature of the material, few of them survive in good condition. Pat Kirkham.

85
Oak chair with chip-carved decoration and pigskin seat designed by Romney Green, most intellectual of craftsmen, c.1925, and possibly made by Stanley Davies, his assistant at the time. Romney Green's furniture, handmade and highly detailed, is always interesting and inventive but, compared with the best of the Cotswold designers, tends to be more self-conscious and over-wrought. Cheltenham Art Gallery and Museum.

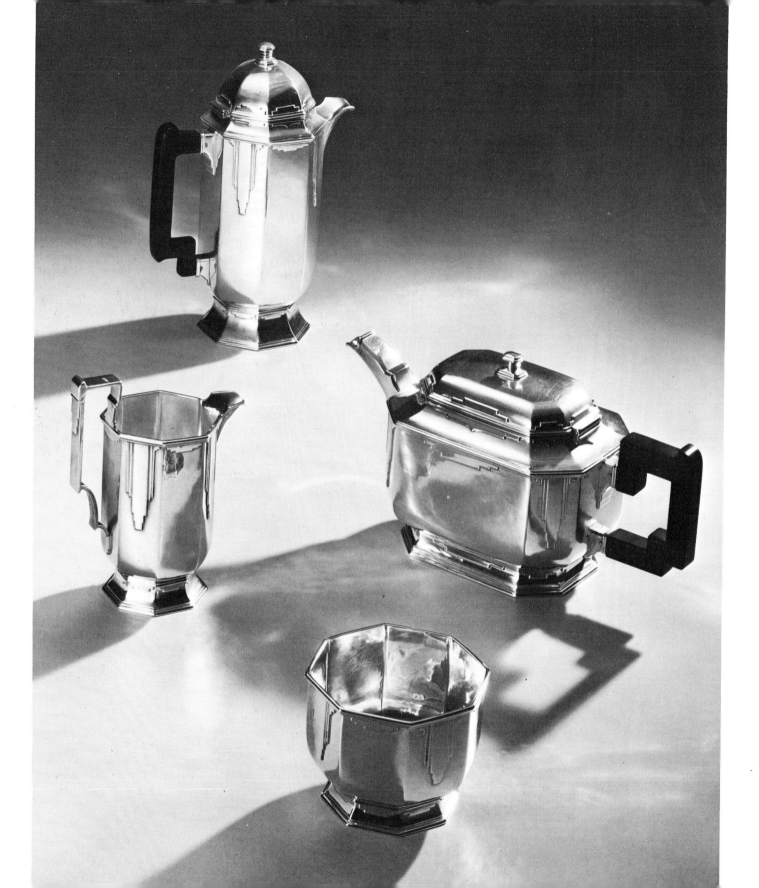

86
Silver tea-set, octagonal in form, designed by Harold Stabler, made by Wakely and Wheeler, 1928. The Worshipful Company of Goldsmiths.

87 (*right*)
Silver sauceboats designed and made by Ramsden and Carr, 1909–10, and engraved, with typical Ramsden ostentation, 'OMAR RAMSDEN ET ALWYN CARR ME FECERUNT'. Ramsden was the most successful craft silversmith – and one of the best showmen – of the century. The output of his workshop was great, its style uneven; but this pair of sauceboats is a superb example. Victoria and Albert Museum.

this body', he writes, 'only recently and I cannot say how much I owe to its early members, men like Harold Stabler, Crofton Gane, Ben Fletcher, Frank Pick, Charles Holden, Ambrose Heal, Noel Carrington, Harry Peach, Hamilton Smith, Herbert Simon, Harold Curwen, Alfred Read and Leslie Mansfield, all of whom were willing to share their experience with a greenhorn.' It was from the DIA, as he soon makes clear, that Russell absorbed many of the ideas and the principles exemplified in his own furniture and propounded, much later, in his propagandist role as Director of the Council of Industrial Design: the notion that the choice of good design instead of shoddy is better for the chooser and better for the nation, which springs from his belief, a moralistic attitude not far removed from Ruskin and the Arts and Crafts philosophers, that quality – quality of design, of material and of workmanship – is 'the outward and visible sign of good health'.

In its pursuit of Efficiency Style, the DIA was extremely energetic on many different fronts. Though its membership was small – only 200 to begin with, only 602 by 1928 – it managed to be relatively influential because it was well organised

and sensible and practical in its campaigns. Its membership was broadly based. The
DIA stalwarts listed by Gordon Russell include architects and shopkeepers, designers,
manufacturers, printers, writers and an educationalist. This set-up tended naturally
to be a bit incestuous: Stabler worked for Pick, Fletcher designed for Peach, Noel
Carrington wrote copy for Heal's catalogues, and Ambrose Heal, DIA retailer par
excellence, purveyed the products of his colleagues. Heal's catalogues from 1918 to
the late 1920s are replete with designs which, if not actually made by DIA members,
would have met with their approval: from the cheerful clean pottery with simple
decoration to the clear crystal glassware, including coloured vases in 'butterfly-wing
blue', and the sensible furniture for people of discernment. There is obvious
avoidance of the showy and the wayward, a contrasting concentration on the
decent and the modest, the pleasant and the comely, the practical and the
workmanlike, well made and well proportioned: public manifestation of the main
DIA tenets, the commercial stamp on DIA right-thinking. How much nearer to need
would it be possible to get?

For the first time in its history, design in Britain had an official, or at least a semi-
official, framework. It was gradually acquiring the first of the committees,
memoranda, conferences, reports, propaganda exhibitions and information bureaux
which feature so prominently, and at times so comically, in its later years. The DIA
membership was at that time particularly orientated towards typography and

90
Ceremonial cigar box, grey shagreen with silver mounts, designed and made by John Paul Cooper, c.1927. The Worshipful Company of Goldsmiths.

91
Silver cigarette box with blue enamel decoration designed by Harold Stabler, 1923. For Stabler, leading member of the DIA, fitness for purpose did not necessarily mean plainness and this large cigarette box shows his interpretation of fitness for purpose on the most luxurious level. The Worshipful Company of Goldsmiths.

92
'Dolphin' bowl in silver, designed and made by Omar Ramsden, 1929. The Worshipful Company of Goldsmiths.

printing, the legacy of its origins in Arts and Crafts, and 'Design and Workmanship in Printing' was the theme of the first DIA exhibition held in London in 1915. Further exhibitions in this early series showed exemplary pottery and textiles; a small exhibition of well-designed furniture was held by the DIA in 1919 in Shoreditch, strategically placed to convert East End manufacturers; a larger 'Exhibition of Household Things' – 'designed', of course, 'primarily to serve their purpose' – was held in Whitechapel in 1920. From 1916 onwards the DIA was publishing spasmodic Journals and Newsletters, and then, from 1922, a series of DIA Yearbooks appeared regularly. These reflect quite interestingly the changing emphasis of DIA reforming instincts in this period: the early concern with individual household objects, from the storage capacities of wardrobes to the pouring qualities of teapots, has by the late 1920s, burgeoned out to include the whole of town and country planning. It has turned into an urge to redesign the whole environment. This was the heyday of Clough Williams-Ellis's well-known *Cautionary Guides*.

Though it was hard for any government department to emulate the emotional commitment, the reforming effervescence, of the DIA in those days, there was plenty of DIA conviction in the pamphlet *Art and Industry* published in 1919 by the Ministry of Reconstruction, containing such DIA-indoctrinated comments as 'Art is indispensable in life and therefore in education and work'. The following year, as a result of this report, the British Institute of Industrial Art was set up in London.

93
'The Sea Beaker', a small silver vase symbolic of the sea, designed by R.M.Y.Gleadowe, made by H.G.Murphy, with exceptionally fine engraving by George Friend, 1929. The Worshipful Company of Goldsmiths.
94
Silver tea-caddy made by A.E.Jones, Birmingham, 1918. On loan to Birmingham City Museums and Art Gallery.
95
Facetted silver mug designed by Edward Spencer for the Artificers' Guild, 1926. The Worshipful Company of Goldsmiths.

96
Earthenware plate and jug with hand-painted decoration designed by Susie Cooper for A.E.Gray, 1929. Before she set up her own pottery, Susie Cooper worked for Gray's, a small firm in Stoke-on-Trent, as a painter and designer. These florals in soft colours, with their dots and multi-banding, are very prophetic of her later work. Manchester City Art Gallery.

97
Silver alms dish designed and made by R.M.Y.Gleadowe
and H.G.Murphy for the Goldsmiths' Hall collection,
1930. The large dish was raised in one piece, with
spectacular pictorial engraving by George Friend. The
Worshipful Company of Goldsmiths.

Stoneware coffee service with deep green speckled glaze,
designed and manufactured by William Moorcroft,
c.1916. A design so simple and cylindrical that it could
quite easily have been mistaken for a late-1950s Design
Centre Award-winner. Victoria and Albert Museum.

This was a permanent exhibition of 'good design', as the DIA would see it, together
with an information service, and although it was rather unconvincing and short-
lived, it set the pattern for government involvement in approving design standards.
In 1920, too, the Federation of British Industries formed an Industrial Art
Committee which gave itself the task of considering 'the question of industrial art in
this country' (a question which recurs as the century progresses). A Designers'
Register and Employment Bureau – again the first of many – was opened by the
Federation of British Industries in 1924.

At this stage of the narrative of design in Britain, the enlarging network of
committees, associations, and institutes, what one might call the mainstream
propaganda movement, can easily camouflage the force and influence of smaller-
scale and more individual enterprises. But one must remember that this was not
only the age of Efficiency Style, it was also a time of its absolute antithesis, a period
of spiritual reassessment and social experiment in which a belief in the regenerative
values of handwork once again loomed large. Nowhere was this more manifest than
at Ditchling, Sussex, in Eric Gill and Hilary Pepler's Guild of St Joseph and
St Dominic, described by Gill, who had himself by then become a Dominican

99
'Harvest' earthenware pattern designed by Frank
Brangwyn for Doulton in 1930. This lushly decorative
free-hand pattern, in greens, blues, pinks, yellows, rich
browns, on honey buff, obviously very closely allied to
Brangwyn's painting, attracted great critical acclaim
when Doulton first produced it but, although the price
was kept 'within the reach of people of quite moderate
means', the pattern was never a commercial success.
Richard Dennis.

Tertiary, as 'primarily a religious fraternity for those who make things with their
hands'. (The Eric Gill view of fitness for purpose, which in the end perhaps is not so
far removed from Pick, is that work should be fit both for one's God and for one's
neighbour: 'Good quality is therefore twofold: work must be good itself and good
for use'.) The idea of the moral worth of handwork and the value of crafts to the
community, in effect the old Ruskinian doctrine, was revived, in a new setting, in
such intellectual-artistic communities of the mid-1920s as Dartington in Devon and
Gregynog, northern Powys, in the life of which a central place was given to music
and the crafts.

In 1920, Bernard Leach, the potter, returned from a long period of study in Japan
to set up his own pottery at St Ives in Cornwall. This, a fresh example of the
reawakened interest in the more metaphysical aspects of design, for Leach returned
immersed in the philosophy of pottery, had an enormous influence on the
development of British twentieth-century ceramics. The first students to be trained
at St Ives were Michael Cardew, Katharine Pleydell-Bouverie and Norah Braden,
all of whom of course became considerable potters in their own right. A comparable
spiritual intensity is obvious in the work and in the teaching of the other major

100
'Amenophis', a furnishing linen designed by Roger Fry
for the Omega Workshops which he founded in 1913,
with Duncan Grant and Vanessa Bell, as a kind of
artists' cooperative, beginning (as he explained at the
outset) with 'those crafts in which painters can most
easily and readily engage': wall decoration, printed
cotonnades, painted silks for curtains and dresses,
painted screens and painted furniture. Of these, the
printed textiles were perhaps the most successful. The
Omega lasted until 1919. Victoria and Albert Museum.

potter of this period, William Staite Murray, an orientalist who was one of the
earliest English converts to Buddhism. In 1925, he was appointed Head of Ceramics
at the Royal College of Art. On the one side from Leach, the deeply convinced
craftsman, on the other from Staite Murray, the emphatic artist-potter, involved
widely with the fine-art movements of his day, one can trace a dual tradition in craft
pottery in Britain: the useful and the abstract, the domestic and the sculptural, a
dichotomy which even now persists.

The mid-1920s were a time of renewed movement in the craft world. Edward

101
Roller-printed furnishing cotton designed by Minnie McLeish in 1929 for Foxton's, one of the most enterprising textile manufacturers of this period. Victoria and Albert Museum.

Barnsley, son of Sidney, the Arts and Crafts woodworker whose furniture was one of the great glories of that period, had opened his own workshop in Petersfield in Hampshire; A.Romney Green, poet, mathematician and social reformer as well as a very innovative craftsman, was by then working in Christchurch; his pupil Stanley Davies, an adherent of Romney Green's theories of 'Structural Design', had by the mid-1920s moved up to the Lake District. Links with the Arts and Crafts movement were still strong. The cluster of craft workshops in and around Ditchling retained, according to C.R.Ashbee (who visited them in 1923), much of the old spirit of the

102
Oak dresser designed by Frank Brangwyn and made by
J.W.Stenning. Many years before his reputation as a
painter was established, Brangwyn had been immersed
in the Arts and Crafts: as a boy, he had worked for
William Morris; he was a lifelong friend of
A.H.Mackmurdo. In his later career, there was a
constant correlation between painting and the
decorative arts. This large, well-proportioned and very
English dresser, designed in the mid-1920s, shows the
Arts and Crafts influence still strong. Private collection.

Guild of Handicraft in Chipping Campden. They included the weaving workshop known as Gospels where Ethel Mairet, most remarkable twentieth-century practitioner and theorist, worked for many years and trained other well-known weavers. In her sphere, her influence was comparable with that of Bernard Leach. Ethel Mairet's husband, Philippe, once one of Ashbee's Guildsmen, set up The New Handworkers' Gallery in Percy Street in London, a characteristic 1920s enterprise; here as well as selling craftwork he admired, such as Michael Cardew's pottery, he distributed craft tracts, for instance his own pamphlet 'The Idea Behind Craftsmanship', Ethel Mairet's view of 'Weaving' and 'A Potter's Outlook' by Bernard Leach. A similarly esoteric London shop which specialised in craftwork, selling among other things, the hand-block printed textiles of the Barron-Larcher partnership, was The Little Gallery in Chelsea, opened by Muriel Rose in 1928.

The craft of silversmithing then, as later, took its impetus mainly from the Worshipful Company of Goldsmiths in London. From 1926, with George Hughes as Art Secretary (a role later taken on by his son, Graham), the Company promoted a long series of competitions and exhibitions of modern silverwork, placing a succession of commissions and stimulating a huge interest in the craft. The silversmith-designers on whom Goldsmiths' Hall, in the late 1920s, focused most attention were John Paul Cooper and H.G.Murphy, both highly original exponents of the craft of silversmithing; R.M.Y.Gleadowe, whose designs for engraving on to silver are surely among the very finest of the period; and Harold Stabler, a versatile designer who had been one of the founders of the DIA. Stabler, an important figure of his day, one of the partners in Carter, Stabler, Adams, saw his role as designing for machine production as well as for handmaking. All through the 1920s, this was quite a usual view.

And in fact it was this very flexibility, the way in which designers, far from being hidebound, moved easily between craft and machine production, which created a free and optimistic climate, encouraging to many of the major developments of the next decade. It was a climate in which the work done by Alec Hunter in the small experimental weaving unit set up in the late 1920s by James Morton of Morton Sundour Fabrics led logically on to the Edinburgh Weavers of the 1930s. A period at which the pottery designer, Susie Cooper, hand-decorating one-off pieces for Gray's Pottery, was acquiring the techniques and the confidence to set up her own firm which very soon became well known. This was the time when Enid Marx, whose early designs were strongly influenced by Barron and Larcher, hand-block printers, with whom she worked as an assistant, began to develop her own original thinking and her interest in craft-into-industrial-design, leading on to her work for London Transport and Utility. It was also the decade in which one sees how Gordon Russell, up till then a craft furniture-maker in the superb Cotswold Arts and Crafts tradition took the first steps towards the machine production which made his firm so famous in the 1930s. With so much activity in such varying directions, the 1920s was a period of magnificent transition, and many of the themes and ideas it generated only find their resolution a good deal later on.

The 1930s

After the fairly even tenor of the 1920s, the 1930s was a decade of sudden, obvious change: a shift of visual style, a change of fundamental attitude. In this period, modernism came to Britain, if not in as extreme a form as it was visible in other parts of Europe, certainly as a positive and vigorous new influence. In the 1930s in Britain, as in the rest of Europe, design and architecture were very much related: this was part of the Modern Movement rationale; design was seen largely as a by-product of building; the industrial designers of the period were mainly architects by training. The 1930s were nothing if not open-minded and this was also a notable decade for the cross-fertilisation of fine art and design. Most remarkable of all, by the end of the decade, was the way in which the work of the élite designers, the contemporary idiom of the progressives, had gradually percolated down and become popular, almost part of the everyday culture of the time.

Traditional English reticence of course was still about; the strong element of craftsmanship continued through the 1930s. But added to this there was awakened social purpose, a revived energy to experiment with new techniques and new materials, particularly the techniques of mass production. Ideas altered. This was partly the result of a whole influx of foreign designers and architects who started work in Britain, some temporarily, some permanently, through the 1930s. The Europeanisation of design was first noted in the *Journal* of the DIA by John C.Rogers in 1928. He described the exhibition of modernist furniture at Waring & Gillow, designed by Serge Chermayeff, as 'by far the best thing yet done in this country', going on to say that it was 'not at all on the lines of those whose creed is the teaching of Gimson and the Barnsleys'. It was this new breed of architect-designers which produced such archetypal products of the 1930s as the Isokon Long Chair, in laminated birchwood; the well-known matt-glazed pottery from Wedgwood; the marvellous succession of modernist rugs. Because by this time the frontiers of design were widening quite rapidly, designers soon became involved in more engineering-orientated projects of the period: adjustable reading lamps are typical, and radio cabinets in bakelite.

Around this time, design first began emerging as an organised profession. The main professional association, the Society of Industrial Artists, was founded in 1930. One must not be misled about that early title (later changed to Society of Industrial Artists and Designers), for its original membership included industrial designers, as we would now describe them, as well as graphic specialists and illustrators. The fact that designers still considered themselves artists is perhaps an

103
Weathered oak desk by Ambrose Heal, with leather-
seated chair in green, 1931. In contrast to Heal's simple
cottage furniture, this desk was marketed as a prestige
piece, a signed edition aimed probably at the rising
businessman: the central cupboard opens to reveal a
telephone. Heal collection, Heal and Son.

indication of the feeling of the time: at that stage, the precise professional status of
designers was rather less clear-cut than it was later to become. The profession was
much smaller and more experimental: the visual sense was seen as multi-purpose;
designers simply tackled any job that came along, graphics, exhibitions, architecture,
products. At the same time, designers had a serious sense of mission: one of the
avowed intentions of the SIA was 'to assemble the resources of design as a vital
factor in British industry'. (The debates on how to do it continued through the
decade.) By 1936 the Royal Society of Arts was discussing the creation of the
distinction Designer for Industry, and two years later the first Royal Designers for
Industry were appointed. These were Douglas Cockerell (for bookbinding), Eric
Gill (for typography), James Hogan (for glass), J.H.Mason (for printing and
typography), H.G.Murphy (for gold and silver), Keith Murray (for glass and
pottery), Tom Purvis (for commercial art), Harold Stabler (for pottery and silver),
Fred Taylor (for commercial art), C.F.A.Voysey (for interior decoration, and
furniture and fabric design), George Sheringham, who died before the day of the
appointment ceremony (for stage and interior decoration and costume and textile
design). The first honorary Royal Designer, E.McKnight Kauffer, was appointed
simultaneously 'for services to Commercial Art', which ranged from his posters to
his esoteric abstract 1930s rugs. A highly individual, eclectic group of people, in
themselves a comprehensive history of British design attitudes.

104
The Isokon Long Chair designed by Marcel Breuer,
originally made in laminated birch in 1936, and still in
production. Jack Pritchard.

105
Tubular steel stacking chairs with canvas seat and back,
designed by Serge Chermayeff for Pel, 1932, and used in
the new Broadcasting House, London. Pel.

106
Chair in laminated birch designed by Gerald Summers
for the Makers of Simple Furniture, c.1934. Victoria and
Albert Museum.
107
The Isokon Penguin Donkey, Mark One, in birch
plywood, designed by Egon Riss, 1939. Jack Pritchard.
108
Isokon nesting tables in birch plywood, designed by
Marcel Breuer, 1936. Jack Pritchard.

109
'Shipton' dressing table and stool in black walnut and
chrome, designed by W.H.Russell for Gordon Russell,
1930. By the 1930s, the Gordon Russell factory was
largely adapted to techniques of mass production; design
work was done mainly by W.H.Russell (not a member of
the family) and by Gordon Russell's architect brother,
R.D.Russell. Museum collection, Gordon Russell.

110
Buffet in macassar ebony and burr walnut, designed by
Serge Chermayeff for Waring & Gillow, 1928. One of the
first examples in Britain of the swishly sophisticated
Continental style which was continued through the
1930s by such designers as Betty Joel, Ian Henderson,
Charles Richter. Royal Pavilion, Art Gallery and
Museums, Brighton.

Through the 1930s, a succession of committees of enquiry, some official, some set up by industry itself, were discussing the whole question of Art and Industry. Its national importance by then had been well recognised. The most far-reaching of these investigations was the one by the Board of Trade committee on Art and Industry, set up in 1931 under Lord Gorell. This led to the formation in 1933 of the Council for Art and Industry. The Chairman was Frank Pick and the Council (popularly known as the Pick Council), with its brief to encourage good design, 'especially in relation to manufactures', was an early blue-print for the post-war Council of Industrial Design. In 1937, on the recommendation of the Pick Council, a National Register of Industrial Art Designers was established by the Board of Trade. This promotional work, the linking up of designers and industrialists, has always been seen by the official propagandists as crucially important and indeed it is still being carried out both by the Design Council and the SIAD. In these and other ways, in particular the preoccupation in the 1930s with designers' education, which, it was felt, should be a lot more realistic, one sees increasingly serious concern with design standards from the point of view of the national economy. Here were the early stages of official design policy as it developed in the years after the War.

Perhaps it seems peculiar that at such a time of acute financial crisis so much attention should have been lavished on the problems of design for industry. But in fact, of course, this is a recurring pattern, as relevant to the 1980s as the 1930s: a crisis (or a war) frequently provides the stimulus to plan ahead, to reassess. In furniture, for instance, the declining market for special one-off pieces in the early 1930s encouraged Gordon Russell to direct the major energies of his firm into design for mass production. With this specific aim, Gordon Russell's brother, R.D.Russell, went to train at the Architectural Association, returning to the Cotswolds to produce a whole series of designs for Gordon Russell Furniture which, although quintessentially British, could compete on the same terms as international modern. In the more uncompromising atmosphere of Hampstead, Jack Pritchard, a young engineer-economist and an intrepid patron of the Modern Movement, had set up a company called Isokon, committed to the idea of promoting buildings, furniture and fittings of a strictly functional modern design. Wells Coates, the architect, was a co-founder of Isokon. Walter Gropius, then a refugee from Nazi Germany, became Controller of Design in the Isokon Furniture Company; Marcel Breuer designed furniture for Isokon; Laszlo Moholy-Nagy designed some of the sales leaflets: this, by far the most convinced attempt in Britain to emulate the

111
Tubular steel-frame dining furniture made by Pel in the mid-1930s for Prudential Assurance. Tubular steel furniture had by this time become popular: Bauhaus austerity combined with Hollywood-style glamour. Victoria and Albert Museum.

112
Walnut dresser with spectacular inlaid pattern, designed by Frank Brangwyn and made by E.Pollard in 1930; one of a whole series of modernist designs for furniture, carpets, textiles, ceramics and glass commissioned from Brangwyn at this period. The contrast with his Arts and Crafts oak dresser of the previous decade, no. 102, is emphatic, and the new sense of 1930s stylishness remarkable in a designer born in 1867. William Morris Gallery, Walthamstow.

113
Silver tea service with wood handle, ivory and wood
finial, designed by Harold Stabler and made by Adie
Brothers, 1935. This modernist tea-set, of which there
was also an electroplated version designed to fit on a
bakelite tray, contrasts interestingly with Stabler's more
Art Deco 1920s service, no 86. Victoria and Albert
Museum.

114
Silver bowl with stepped-up lid and ribbed ivory finial,
designed and made by H.G.Murphy, 1936. This
decorative use of ivory with silver was very much in
fashion with the 1930s silversmiths. The Worshipful
Company of Goldsmiths.

115
Tall fluted silver vase, one of a set of six by
R.M.Y.Gleadowe and H.G.Murphy, 1935. The Worshipful Company of Goldsmiths, (as 116, 117 and 118).
116
Small silver box with jet and ivory handle, designed and
made by Cyril Shiner, 1933.
117
Silver bowl with niello decoration, designed and made
by Bernard Cuzner, 1933.
118
Silver tea-caddy with ivory knop, designed by
A.E.Harvey and made by Hukin & Heath, 1933.

international rationalist movement, was memorably satirised by Osbert Lancaster as Twentieth Century Functional style. The Isokon Long Chair, in intellectual circles, had a distinct cachet, but in terms of popular success was soon outdone by the ubiquitous Pel tubular steel stacking chair with canvas seat and back, shortly to be found in every village hall in England, achieving a renown and instant recognition perhaps comparable only with the Hille polypropylene chair of the early 1960s.

In 1932, Alastair Morton, son of James Morton, first became involved in directing an experimental textile unit within the large Morton Sundour firm. This became famous as Edinburgh Weavers, whose fabrics form another potent image of the 1930s. In his role as artistic director, Alastair Morton, himself a painter with many artist friends, with modernist ideals of relating art and architecture, commissioned an extraordinary collection of textiles, perhaps the most remarkable to be produced this century: the 'Constructivist Fabrics' launched in 1937 included designs by Ben Nicholson, Ashley Havinden and Barbara Hepworth. Hans Aufseer, Marion Dorn and John Tandy were also designing regularly for Edinburgh Weavers at this period. Meanwhile, Alec Hunter, Alastair Morton's predecessor at Edinburgh Weavers in its very early days, had by now moved on to Warner's in Braintree, where, as production manager, he acted as controller of design and encouraged the development, in 1935, of a department for exclusive handwoven fabrics under the weaver Theo Moorman. Another influential figure of 1930s textile design was Allan Walton, architect and painter and interior decorator as well as director of his own textile manufacturing firm: he too commissioned textile designs from well-known artists of the period. (He was about to be appointed Professor of Textiles at the Royal College of Art when, in 1948, he died.) Two important freelance textile designers came to work in Britain in the 1930s: Margaret Leischner, a hand-weaver from the Bauhaus, and Marianne Straub, whose industrial experience in her native Switzerland was augmented by the time she spent with Ethel Mairet in her hand-weaving workshop in Ditchling, Sussex. Both these designers remained to work in Britain in the post-war period, strengthening the tradition of hand and machine.

119
'Ridgeway' cutlery, silverplate, made by Roberts and
Belk, c.1935. Lent by Sheffield City Museums.
120
Coffee-set in earthenware, with white 'Moonstone' glaze,
designed by Keith Murray for Wedgwood, c.1934. Keith
Murray's background as an architect perhaps accounts
for his coolness and precision: his was the very opposite
of craftsman's pottery. Victoria and Albert Museum.

121
Early morning tea-set in earthenware, black and brown
on a grey ground, made by Poole Pottery, about 1937.
The 'Streamline' shape was designed by John Adams,
the pattern by Truda Carter. Victoria and Albert
Museum.

China plate with the 'Mayfair' decoration designed by Milner Gray for E.Brain (Foley China), 1935. An elegant example of nostalgic witticism which tempered British modernism at this period. Milner Gray.

In 1931, Susie Cooper moved her pottery firm, founded two years earlier, into its permanent home, the Crown Works, Burslem. Here too the interaction of hand and machine – for instance, the use of both hand-painting and lithographic techniques for decoration – was much in evidence all through the 1930s, a period of considerable success for Susie Cooper. (Even Queen Mary bought a Susie Cooper tea-set.) Susie Cooper's 'Kestrel' shape with 'washband' decoration, 'Polka Dot' and 'Wedding Ring'; Poole Pottery's 'Streamline' with its two-tone 'Mushroom' glazes; the 'Vogue' and 'Mode' shapes produced by Shelley Potteries: such developments as these, so evocative of their particular period, had an obvious effect on the industry in general. Some of the most progressive designs were emanating from the Wedgwood factory, where Victor Skellern was appointed Art Director in 1934. The design pundits of the time praised Keith Murray, the architect (who also designed glass for Stevens and Williams and silver for Mappin and Webb) for his very rational matt-glazed Wedgwood pottery: 'better', said Herbert Read of the

123
Decanter and glass designed by Keith Murray for Stevens & Williams, c.1935. Another good example (cf. no. 120) of Keith Murray's architectural approach to tableware. He also designed very successfully in metal. Leicestershire Museums.

124
'Cactus' cut-glass vase, designed by Keith Murray for Stevens & Williams, c.1938. The cactus was of course at the time a well-known feature of the modernist interior: (see Osbert Lancaster, Homes Sweet Homes, 'now the cactus sprouts where once flourished the aspidistra and the rubber plant'). Manchester City Art Gallery.

matt-straw Wedgwood beer mug, 'than anything else in modern ceramics'. Many of Wedgwood's major decorative designs were the work of the artist and illustrator Eric Ravilious, in his picturesque, affectionate and very English style. In glass, some particularly interesting pieces were developed for Chance, for industrial production, by Robert Goodden, the architect-designer, whose 'Asterisk' wallpaper was also a beautifully characteristic pattern of that time

One of the most striking advances in the 1930s was the increased involvement of designers in industrial product design: not just in the traditional craft-orientated areas of furniture, textiles, ceramics, glass and so on, but also, gradually, in the newer technology-based industries. There was, for instance, a sudden influx of designer-designed radios: E.K.Cole commissioned new radio cabinets in plastics from Serge Chermayeff, Wells Coates and Misha Black, while Murphy developed a now classic range of cabinets in wood with Gordon and Dick Russell. As Gordon Russell records in his autobiography, these were planned to reflect function, designed

125
Upholstery moquette designed for London Passenger
Transport Board by Enid Marx, 1937. The designer's
brief was exacting: strong contrasting tones had to be
used to keep the seat cover looking fresh after hard
wear; but the design must avoid dazzling the passengers
in moving vehicles. The scale of the repeat was dictated
by the economics of cutting out the fabric for differently-
sized seats. Enid Marx.

126
'Fugue' screen-printed linen designed by Paul Nash,
1936. Victoria and Albert Museum.

127
Upholstery moquette designed by Enid Marx for London
Passenger Transport Board, 1937. Enid Marx.

116

'Vogue' lightweight suitcase in cowhide, designed by
John Waterer for S.Clarke & Co., manufacturers of
Watajoy Luggage, c.1937. Note the innovative zipper
fastening. An interesting example of designers'
involvement in new areas of product design in the 1930s;
patterned linings for John Waterer's luggage were
purpose-designed by Enid Marx. Leathercraft collection,
Northampton Museum.

from the inside outwards: a DIA-inspired fundamentalist approach which, at that
period, was very far from usual. In terms of what came later, as industrial design for
engineering was developed, the products of the 1930s seem very small beginnings: a
convector heater here, an Anglepoise light there. But they were important, not only
because of the intrinsic quality of some of the finest 1930s design solutions, but also
as proof of the designer's capabilities, his value to society. More and more, this
began to be recognised by industry: for instance, by Troughton & Young, the
lighting manufacturers, who had now appointed A.B.Read, a Royal College-trained
designer, as their Design Director. It was also the conviction behind the formation
of the first of the corporate design groups in the 1930s. In 1935, the Bassett Gray
partnership, founded by Milner Gray and Charles and Henry Bassett in the early
1920s and at that time mainly preoccupied with graphics, reconstituted itself as a
new group, Industrial Design Partnership, with enlarged emphasis on product
design. Misha Black, one of the partners, was to be a crucial figure in the immense

129
Ekco radio cabinet in bakelite, designed by Wells
Coates, winner of competition for a modern plastics
wireless cabinet organised by E.K.Cole in 1932. This
design, which has become almost a symbol of the 1930s,
was first brought out in 1934, in walnut brown and
black; later it was also made in ivory and onyx. Patrick
Cook.
130
Ecko radio cabinet in bakelite, designed by Serge
Chermayeff and first made by E.K.Cole in 1934. Besides
designs by Wells Coates and Serge Chermayeff, E.K.Cole
produced wireless cabinets by Jesse Collins, in 1936, and
Misha Black, in 1938. Patrick Cook.

131
Electric convector heater with chromed finish, designed
by Christian Barman for HMV, 1934. Victoria and
Albert Museum.
132
Radio cabinet in light walnut designed by R.D.Russell
for Murphy Radio, 1937. Perhaps the best of the long
line of Murphy cabinets, mass-produced by Gordon
Russell through the 1930s, which had so obvious an
influence on the design-awareness of other
manufacturers. Museum collection, Gordon Russell.

133
Thermovent electric convector heater designed by Wells
Coates for E.K.Cole in 1937. Several versions of this
heater were produced, in dark brown or black plastic,
and production continued for some years after the war.
Victoria and Albert Museum.

134
Anglepoise lamp designed for Herbert Terry by
G.Carwardine in 1932. The idea was a simple one: for a
lamp based on the mechanism of the human arm,
infinitely adjustable. The Anglepoise, little altered, is still
in production, and makes an unfailing appearance in all
exhibitions of design classics. Science Museum.
135
The Bestlite was designed by R.D.Best for his family
firm, Best & Lloyd of Birmingham, 1930. Though
evidently inspired by Bauhaus principles, this lamp has
a trace of traditionalism which ends up by making its
appearance very English: in its time, it was much
admired by the pundits, and like the Anglepoise, no. 134,
the Bestlite is still in production. Museum collection,
Gordon Russell.

post-war expansion of design for engineering. Industrial Design Partnership later
developed into Design Research Unit, the leading design group in Britain in the
years after the War.

The 1930s was a memorable time for design patronage. Designers, later on, came
to look back with nostalgia on the early design entrepreneurs, such strong
enthusiasts as Alastair Morton at Edinburgh Weavers; Frank Murphy of Murphy
Radio; Jack Pritchard and Isokon. Frank Pick, appointed in 1933 Vice-Chairman
and Chief Executive of the London Passenger Transport Board, was an almost
legendary design patron of the 1930s; London Transport design policy became a
kind of marvel, the envy of artistic foreign visitors to Britain. And all through the

136
'Tree of Life', left, and 'Spirals', right: two earthenware patterns designed by Susie Cooper and first produced in 1938. Susie Cooper Pottery.

137
Electric fire designed by Wells Coates for Jack and Molly Pritchard's own apartment in Lawn Road Flats. Hampstead, 1934. University of East Anglia Collection.

decade, a time described in retrospect by Enid Marx as 'that halcyon period when all the arts flowered in such profusion', new patrons were emerging. For instance, Colin Anderson, a young director in his family shipping firm, the Orient Line, commissioned not only new ships – the *Orion*, 1935 and the *Orcades*, 1937 – but also a whole range of new interior fittings, from the carpets to the cutlery, substantial orders in a firmly modern idiom which helped to set new standards in the corresponding industries.

Essential patrons of design in the 1930s were the shopkeepers. In 1929, Gordon Russell's firm had opened a shop in Wigmore Street which sold, as well as furniture from Broadway, a whole collection of related products such as textiles, glass and pottery; from 1936 there was a larger shop as well, a few doors down the street, where for several years the merchandise was chosen by Nikolaus Pevsner, the art historian, a recent refugee from Nazi Germany. Another influential individual shop was Dunbar Hay, opened by Cecilia Dunbar Kilburn (later Lady Sempill) and Athole Hay in Grosvenor Street. Dunbar Hay was especially successful in promoting the work of Eric Ravilious and other staff and students from the Royal College of Art in London, where Athole Hay was Registrar. New designs were being encouraged by such Modern-Movement furnishers as Gane's of Bristol, early patron of Marcel Breuer, and Dunn's of Bromley in the pre-war pioneering days of Geoffrey Dunn. In 1938, Dunn, Crofton Gane and Gordon Russell formed the Good Furniture Group, a small association of enterprising retailers – 'a few real believers', as Dunn later described them – who commissioned designs and had them

'Polka Dot', 'Exclamation Mark', and 'Wedding Ring': three tableware designs, moderately modern and generally popular, produced by Susie Cooper at her pottery in Burslem in the early 1930s. Susie Cooper Pottery.

139
'Crayon Swirl' decoration on 'Curlew' shape earthenware, designed and manufactured by Susie Cooper from 1935. Susie Cooper Pottery.

manufactured. By this time, a number of modern design tendencies, especially the vogue for unit furniture, began coming into evidence in some of the large stores.

In the 1930s, the scene seemed to be beginning to be set for the 'new spirit of design' which had been prophesied for the past half century. By the mid-1930s, the idea had been well publicised by a whole succession of books and exhibitions, most notably at Dorland Hall in 1933. Modern design had become a much-used concept, the subject of discussion programmes on the BBC. The modern design movement had acquired its own philosophers, the most widely read of whom was Herbert Read, whose classic *Art and Industry*, published in 1934, was seized on both as handbook and as bible by the modernists. The rational aesthetic, the minimalist outlook – always tempered by a British moderation and good humour – was just about beginning to be seen to be convincing. It is tempting to speculate about the course of history had it not been for the intervention of the War.

The 1940s and 1950s

At the end of World War II, in the general mood of hope for a regenerated nation, two developments took place, both of which soon proved of particular importance to design in Britain: the formation, in 1944, of the Council of Industrial Design (now known as the Design Council); and the reorganisation of the Royal College of Art by Robin Darwin, appointed Principal in 1948. After the War, as a symptom of the idealistic socialism of the time, the main preoccupation was design for mass production, the idea of good design for the great mass of British people. An almost euphoric sense of optimism, stimulated by the Festival of Britain, is discernible in much of post-war design thinking, as the design profession gathered strength.

The character of British design was altered brusquely as the pre-war 1930s experimental style which, however rational, had had a kind of glamour, a self-confident urbanity, gave way to the unadulterated plainness of Utility, in which the back-to-basics idiom had been dictated as much by sheer shortage of materials as by any intellectual functionalist theories. Utility style has an obvious solemnity, almost a kind of smugness, as of Arts and Crafts austerity pushed to its utmost limit. Perhaps as a result, the post-war *volte-face*, Festival style as it soon came to be described in a tone of affectionate nostalgia, was determinedly lightweight, more self-consciously flippant. The element of whimsy which crept in in the 1950s can be beautifully observed in such Festivaliana as the Race Antelope chairs and the crystal-structure textiles, and it carries on through to the end of the decade to the classic early collections of Design Centre Awards.

In October 1942, the first Utility Furniture was shown to the public at the Building Centre. From then on until several years after War had ended, Utility was the only furniture permitted to be made in Britain. The Utility episode is so significant not just because of the historic antecedents of the Utility style, its origins in Arts and Crafts and DIA right-thinking, but also because it was a quite unprecedented example of state intervention in regulating standards of design. The chief influence, indeed to some extent the mastermind, behind Utility was Gordon Russell, first a member of the Board of Trade's Advisory Committee on Utility Furniture and then, from 1943, the Chairman of its newly-appointed Design Panel. The brief, to ensure 'a supply of furniture of the best quality available, at controlled prices, to meet a real need' was, it seemed to some (including Gordon Russell), a rare chance for reforming by example of what was possible in the least auspicious circumstances. Utility appeared an almost godsent opportunity to raise the whole level of national design standards. Arguments are still in progress, almost forty

140
Utility furniture prescribed by the Board of Trade in World War II: the dining chair, designed in 1942, was included in the original Utility catalogue; the 'Cotswold' dining table, in mahogany or oak, was introduced in 1946. Geffrye Museum.

141
Utility tallboy chest in light oak, 1942. Gordon Russell was an original member of the Board of Trade Advisory Committee on Utility Furniture, later Chairman of the Design Panel, and many Utility designs show a remarkable stylistic similarity to Russell's early pieces: compare this Utility tallboy with Russell's own tallboy chest of the mid-1920s, no. 79. Geffrye Museum.

years later, about how well Utility in fact succeeded: were the standards too high-minded, or were they perhaps too lenient? But what, in retrospect, seems altogether clear, is that Utility design was a successful expression, a convincing affirmation, of the standards of British commonsense and moderation which Gordon Russell could be seen wholeheartedly pursuing a few years later as Director of the Council of Industrial Design. By the time that Utility furniture production ended officially in 1952, there was some regret, even in trade circles which had at the beginning been bitterly opposed to it. Since, because of the stringency of the regulations it was practically impossible to produce a shoddy piece of furniture, Utility had by then, ironically in view of the shortage of materials and labour, gained a widespread reputation for quality. Aspects of its appearance, its sensible proportions, its sturdy masculinity, its total lack of flashiness, had an obvious impact on modern British furniture of the post-war period.

The Council of Industrial Design came into being at the end of the War, December 1944, as a result of the Weir Report on Industrial Design and Art in Industry made to the Post-War Export Trade Committee of the Department of Overseas Trade. The Council was established as a grant-aided body financed by the Board of Trade, and the fact that it was founded by a coalition government, independent of inter-

142
Oak sideboard, designed in the post-Utility period between 1948 and 1951, when restrictions had been partially lifted and manufacturers were allowed to design their own furniture within the Utility guidelines. Geffrye Museum.

143
Dining chair in pre-cast aluminium designed by Ernest Race for Race Furniture, 1945. These chairs, designed with great ingenuity in the years of post-war shortage, when conventional materials were strictly limited, were shown in the 'Britain Can Make It' exhibition and continued in production until 1969. Sally Race.

party policies, was to stand it in good stead in later years. The first Director was S.C.Leslie, followed by Gordon Russell in 1947; the commitment of the Council was, broadly, 'to promote by all practicable means the improvement of design in the products of British industry'. In spite of its small size – it began with just ten staff – and in spite of the misgivings of contemporary free-thinkers who resented the idea of government intervention in aesthetics, the Council set about its vast task with zest and confidence which, from this distance, seems both touching and amazing. The early publications of the Council, patient and painstaking in their exposition, are full of earnest visions of a better-designed Britain, a country made more practical, for the man at his work, more dignified and pleasant for the woman in her kitchen, for the children in their schools. Perhaps, in a sense, it had all been said before. The aims and statements of the Council of Industrial Design were quite familiar to the veterans of the many past design campaigns. The middle-of-the-road ideals and principles reflected a whole history of British design attitudes through the years of propaganda from the early DIA to the Pick Council of the 1930s. But because it was official and, as it enlarged, was quite generously financed, the Council of Industrial Design was more effective than its predecessors in propagating the views which it believed in, and the opportunities it was to open out for post-war

125

'Antelope' chair with bent plywood seat and steel rod
frame, designed by Ernest Race for Race Furniture,
1951. The 'Antelope', which came to fame at the Festival
of Britain, is shown here with its original ball feet, so
perfectly characteristic of the period. James Hamilton.

British designers were enormous. As it developed, it was to be the model for design
organisations throughout the world.

Early on in the Council's life, in 1946, it was asked to stage a major exhibition,
ambitiously intended 'To intensify the interest of manufacturers and distributors in
industrial design and their awareness of the desirability of rapid progress; to arouse
greater interest in design in the minds of the general public, as consumers; and to
stage a prestige advertisement before the world for British industry, industrial
design and standards of display'. This exhibition was 'Britain Can Make It', the
first major government-sponsored exhibition of design ever to be held, colloquially
known as 'Britain Can't Have It', since many exhibits, at a time of great austerity,
were either prototypes or being made for export only. Though many doubts were
cast on the wisdom of Sir Stafford Cripps, then President of the Board of Trade, in
insisting that this was a propitious or even a practical time to display British
achievement in industrial design, his judgment was vindicated by the usefulness of
the exhibition in assessing the national potential in design and in setting the

145
Wing settee designed by Ernest Race for Race Furniture, 1948. With its companion chair, this button-backed design – modern but far from outrageous – was a favourite choice for many middle-brow interiors. Robert Race.

146
'Hillestak' chair with moulded plywood seat and back, designed by Robin Day for Hille, 1957. Royal Pavilion, Art Gallery and Museums, Brighton.

147
Convertible bed-settee designed by Robin Day for Hille
in 1957 and included that same year in the first selection
of Design Centre Awards. Amstad Systems.

148
Mahogany sideboard with Bombay rosewood veneer,
designed by David Booth for Gordon Russell, 1951. The
machine-cut decoration – a routed groove exposing the
white birch below – is typically 1950s. Douglas
Barrington.

149
Mahogany dining chair with leather upholstery designed
by Ronald Carter for the Royal College of Art Senior
Common Room, 1951. Ronald Carter.
150
Mahogany dining chair designed by W.H.Russell for
Gordon Russell in 1949 and in continuous production
ever since. Its success stems, perhaps, from its
unobtrusive confidence, its style of moderation, even
from its touch of dullness: qualities of the British
tradition through the ages. Gordon Russell.

dialogue in motion between the Council and many British industries. For 'Britain Can Make it', 3,385 manufacturers were contacted and 1,297 were chosen to exhibit. Altogether, 5,259 products were selected to be shown at the Victoria and Albert Museum in settings specially designed by James Gardner, Chief Exhibition Designer, his assistant Basil Spence, Robert Goodden, Misha Black and others (many of whom were to reassemble later as designers for the Festival of Britain). Most of all, Sir Stafford Cripps' idea in staging such a large-scale exhibition was justified by the public response, which was both unexpected and extraordinary. Contemporary photographs show people queuing in their hundreds down Cromwell Road to see it. In its fourteen-week run, 'Britain Can Make It' was visited by 1,432,546 members of the public, sixty per cent under forty. This dawning public interest in a modern design idiom – 'contemporary style' as it soon came to be depicted – was, once again, a foretaste of the Festival of Britain, five years later.

'Britain Can Make It' was the very first attempt, on any serious level, to put over to the public the idea of the designer; it identified the designer's special skills, the combined attributes of artist, scientist and technician which make the contribution of the designer so essential to the process of industrial development. The traditional rift in British education between the arts and sciences, the cerebral and practical, academic as opposed to visually-based training, had been analysed and deprecated by Robin Darwin, Education Officer of the Council of Industrial Design, in his report on the training of designers in 1946. When, two years later, Robin Darwin was appointed Principal of the Royal College of Art in London he had a unique

151
'Oriana' jugs in stainless steel designed by Robert Welch, originally for the Orient Line, and manufactured by Old Hall, 1958. Robert Welch trained as a craft silversmith, but from the mid-1950s his work in stainless steel became equally important. The Worshipful Company of Goldsmiths.

152
Silver teapot from tea and coffee service designed by Robert Goodden for the Royal Pavilion at the Festival of Britain, 1951. A resplendent example of the strain of eccentricity and fantasy in British design tradition. The four component pieces are engraved with rhyming couplets, each, according to the designer, who also wrote the poetry, making a play on the unlikely meeting of the Sea and Tea. Victoria and Albert Museum.

153
'Pride' silverplated cutlery with white xylonite knife handles, designed by David Mellor for Walker & Hall, 1954. The design was included in the first set of Design Centre Awards in 1957 and is still in production. David Mellor.

chance to reverse many of these tendencies, with a success which is by now almost a legend. His determined revitalisation of the College, which after the War was in a state of disarray; his appointment of a sequence of Professors who were themselves experienced architects and/or designers; his clear sense of the purpose of the College as primarily an institution for the training of designers for industry: all this, in its day, was so effective that by the late 1950s, a good proportion of RCA-trained designers were occupying key positions as staff designers, mainly in the craft-based industries, or else were setting up their own design consultancies. In the 1950s, on the model of design in Scandinavia, these were mainly on a small and personal scale.

The year of the Festival of Britain, 1951, was a landmark for British architecture and design. National events focused on four main areas: arts, science, technology and industrial design. The South Bank exhibition, the centre of attention, proved effectively to many disbelieving critics that modern design could be a popular success. In a corporate-image exercise on a hitherto unprecedented scale, the Council of Industrial Design was empowered to co-ordinate design throughout the Festival. The Council was responsible for all the manufactured objects included in the Festival, in all 10,000 products, and no smallest detail, from the litter bins and signposts to the cafe chairs and tables seems to have escaped its official surveillance. It was a job which delighted Gordon Russell, with his strong convictions that design was omnipresent in a civilised society, that design should be a facet of ordinary living. One especially typical Festival development, poignant in its mixture of earnestness and levity, was the series of decorative patterns promoted by the Council through the Festival Pattern Group: these were applied to such products as textiles, lighting fittings, dinner plates and wine glasses, and were the forerunners of innumerable experiments in patterning and texturing in the immediate post-Festival period (the war-time restrictions on decoration were finally lifted in 1952). But beyond the crystal-structure fabrics, the splayed legs and the ball finials, the Festival ephemera, there were some more fundamental signs of influence: a solid core of interest in the idea of design management and a new concern with standards of environment and the designer's role in attempting to control them, preoccupations which reappear so constantly in the ideologies of the next two decades.

In this post-war period, design became a cult. The publicity it attracted was enormous. But one must remember that, compared with later developments in British design history, the aims and actual achievements of the movement were, at this stage, at least up to the mid-1950s, relatively limited and narrow. It was still very much a pioneering period, still very much a matter of individual enterprise. The scene was dominated by descendants of the early DIA progressives, by people with a cause. One of these was Ernest Race, the furniture designer, who from 1945 was Director of Design for Race Furniture Ltd, an engineering-orientated company producing the most innovative of post-war British furniture. Another important post-war pioneer was Hille, an old-established East End manufacturer of furniture which, in 1949, commissioned its first designs from Robin Day, beginning a historic collaboration. At Edinburgh Weavers, from the mid-1950s onwards, reflecting the relief at the ending of restrictions, Alastair Morton commissioned the now famous series of large artist-designed abstract textile patterns which were so true to the feeling of that time.

131

155
Stainless steel toast-rack designed by Robert Welch for
Old Hall, 1955. Robert Welch.

156
Stainless steel nutcrackers designed by Robert Welch for
Old Hall, 1958. The Worshipful Company of Goldsmiths.

154 (*left*)
Silver coffee-pot designed and made by Gerald Benney,
1957. The tall tapered cylinder form much cultivated by
the craft silversmiths of the late 1950s, was just as
popular with the pottery designers of the period, see
no. 157. The Worshipful Company of Goldsmiths.

157
Spode 'Apollo' bone-china tableware, designed by Neal
French and David White, then Royal College of Art
students, and produced by W.T.Copeland in 1959. The
following year Spode 'Apollo' won the Duke of
Edinburgh's annual Prize for Elegant Design. The Spode
Museum.

158
'Heartsease' tableware pattern, in black and shades of purple, designed by Edward Bawden for the Orient Line and manufactured by Wedgwood, 1952. The artist Edward Bawden had been producing decorative designs for pottery since the mid-1920s, when he designed for Carter Stabler Adams; 'Heartsease' shows a fastidious and sophisticated treatment of many of the decorative motifs popular at the time of the Festival of Britain. Cecil Higgins Art Gallery, Bedford.

In stimulating public awareness of design, the rash of small design shops of the late 1940s and 1950s was important. These reflected their proprietors' own conscientious choice and set a kind of standard for household style and judgment which one can see leading inexorably on to the Habitat stores of the later 1960s. The first of these highly personal small shops of the early post-war period was Primavera in Sloane Street in London, opened in 1945 by Henry Rothschild. It gained a reputation for its modern textiles and also, increasingly, for its British craft work, an area of design which, although eclipsed in the post-war concentration on design for mass production, would soon be re-emerging.

'I am never for forcing the pace', wrote Gordon Russell in his days at the Council of Industrial Design: limited advance and then consolidation was his motto, and

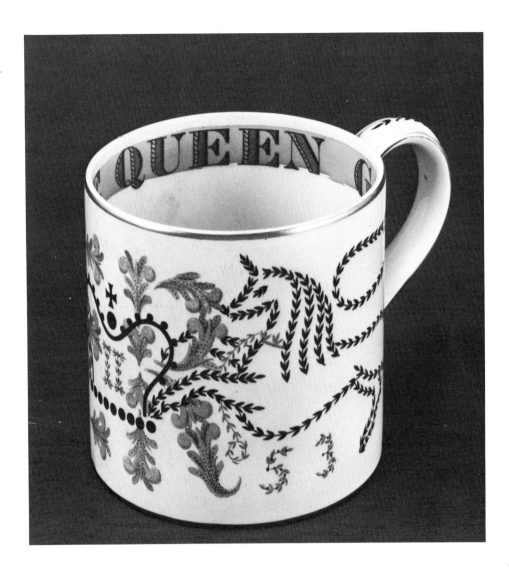

this sums up very nicely the feeling of the period, high-minded and low-key, perhaps
a bit self-congratulatory, as Design Week followed Design Week, as *Design* magazine
began its publication, and as design standards for 'consumer goods', the furniture
and fabrics, the pottery and glassware, the cooking pots and lighting fittings which
at this period were the Council's major target, slowly but undeniably improved. In
1956, the Design Centre was opened in the Haymarket in London, followed the
next year by the Design Centre in Glasgow. In 1957, the first of the Design Centre
Awards were given to such exemplary products as Melmex plastic tableware and
Rayburn room-heaters, as fit for their purpose as could be. The early batches of
Design Centre Awards, which at the time attracted public interest on a scale
unimaginable later, helped greatly to consolidate the reputations of the new RCA-

135

160
Shallow bowl in stoneware with sgraffito decoration, c.1954. Lucie Rie had arrived in England from Vienna in 1938, and in the post-war period, together with Hans Coper, she quite rapidly established a new tradition in craft pottery in Britain, in many ways the opposite to that of Leach and Cardew. Leicestershire Museums.

161
'Mandala' Wilton carpet designed by Audrey Tanner for Carpet Manufacturing Co., 1959. This pattern, an early Design Centre Award-winner, was one of the most widely-used carpets of its period, to be found in innumerable hotel foyers, cinemas and contemporary-style conference halls. Victoria and Albert Museum.

162
'Piazza' plastics-coated fabric designed by Eddie Pond
for Bernard Wardle, 1958. Eddie Pond.

163
'Royal Gobelin' Axminster carpet designed by Neville and Mary Ward
for Tomkinson's, 1958. Victoria and Albert Museum.

164
'Impasto' wallpaper designed by Audrey Levy for The
Wallpaper Manufacturers, 1956. Audrey Levy.
165
'Calyx' screen-printed linen designed by Lucienne Day
for Heal Fabrics, 1951. The Whitworth Art Gallery,
University of Manchester.

166
Bus shelter, galvanised steel with vitreous-enamelled
panels, designed by David Mellor for Abacus, 1957.
Abacus Municipal.

167
'Prestwick' leather suitcases designed by K.H.Paterson
for S.E.Norris, 1957. Victoria and Albert Museum.

168
Street light designed by Richard Stevens for Atlas
Lighting, 1959. From the late 1950s, as the Council of
Industrial Design began to involve itself increasingly in
engineering design, the sphere of influence for
professional designers enlarged greatly: see especially the
area referred to rather picturesquely as 'street furniture'.
Lantern, Victoria and Albert Museum; lighting column,
Abacus Municipal.

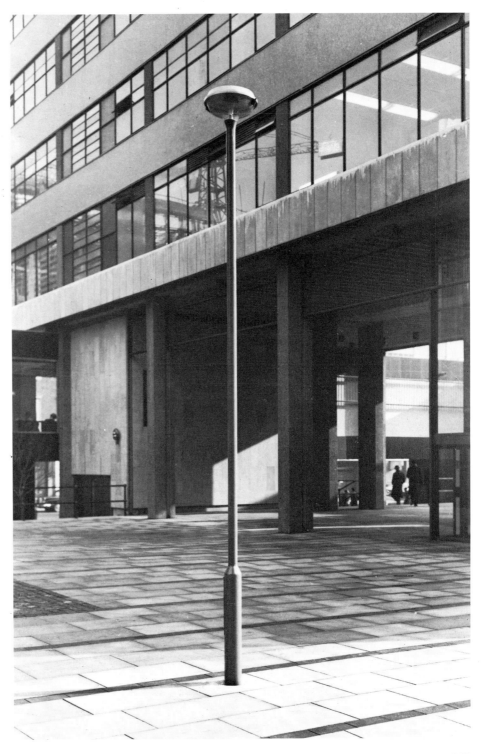

169
Television set designed by Robin Day for Pye, 1957.
Victoria and Albert Museum.
170
Chair in beech, designed by Christopher Heal in the
semi-Utility period, 1948–51. Geffrye Museum.

171
Jewel casket in black leather, designed by John Waterer,
1956. Leathercraft collection, Northampton Museum.

172
'Rayburn' solid fuel heater, designed by David Ogle for
Allied Ironfounders, 1956. Victoria and Albert Museum.

173
Bedside clock in copper with synchronous movement,
designed by Jack Howe for Gent & Co., 1948. Jack Howe.

trained designers and the companies they worked for: David Mellor and Walker & Hall cutlery, Robert Heritage and Archie Shine furniture, Robert Welch and Old Hall stainless steel.

The early post-war scene was gentlemanly, rather cosy, not so far away from the Arts and Crafts in atmosphere. But by the late 1950s, there were signs of growth and change and a much-enlarging area of influence for designers. This was partly the result of COID initiative, its growing involvement in design for capital goods: the first of a series of COID conferences, 'Industrial Design and the Engineering Industries', was held in Birmingham in 1958, and *Design* magazine was by this time including regular reviews of engineering products, stressing the role of the industrial designer as an integral member of the development team and emphasising the designer's potential contribution not only to the visual aspects of the equipment, its final appearance, but also to its practicality in use, the areas defined as the ergonomic factors. Ergonomics was a term which came into constant use, and as the campaign grew for the employment of designers, trained in visual perception and ergonomic skills, in the development of heavy engineering machinery and equipment and such areas as large-scale transport projects, the historic names of Stephenson, Brunel and Fowler, designers on a massive scale, were frequently invoked.

By the late 1950s, too, the role of the designer was beginning to be recognised within the public sector. It began to be seen as an important factor both in its direct benefits to the quality of life of the community and in its usefulness in public image-building. The airport authorities had, by this time, become convinced users of designers' services, a policy which still continues. British Railways, in 1956, established its Design Panel, appointing its first Director of Design. London Transport, too, was advised by a Design Panel, though it never again quite achieved the standards of coherence set for it, single-handed, by Frank Pick. From the 1950s onwards, the Ministry of Public Building and Works (later the Department of the Environment) pursued a systematic design policy, both in employing its own designers and commissioning designs from outside specialists. The Ministry of Transport, in an interesting example of attempted political control of visual standards, subsidised the lighting on trunk roads on condition that the authorities concerned had selected their lighting columns from those pre-approved by the COID.

The whole pattern of designing in Britain could be seen to be altering, subtly and gradually. The relative amateurism of the 1930s and the early post-war period, the small-scale, very personal, often craft-orientated design offices, working along Scandinavian lines, were soon to be overtaken by much larger, multi-purpose, more Americanised design consultancies. The first of these, Design Research Unit, had been founded in 1942 with the intention of presenting 'a service so complete that it could undertake any design case which might confront the State, Municipal Authorities, Industries or Commerce'. Under its leading co-partners, Misha Black and Milner Gray, it had flourished in the intervening period, benefiting from 'Britain Can Make It' and the Festival, dominating corporate design practice in Britain until the mid-1950s when, in the prevailingly expansionist mood, the sense of increasing possibilities in large-scale designing, other equally ambitious design combines began emerging. These included Ogle, founded in 1954, which quickly

174
'Knifecut' pruner designed by Hulme Chadwick for Wilkinson Sword, 1956. Wilkinson Sword.

Mini Minor designed by Alec Issigonis for British Motor
Corporation and first produced in 1959. Sturdy,
functional, trim, tidy, unpompous, rather jolly: by the
mid-1960s the Mini, then world-famous, had become
almost synonymous with the best in British design.
British Leyland Heritage collection.

acquired its current reputation as the most professional transport design consultancy;
Conran, which began in 1955 with furniture and fabrics, shops and exhibitions; and
Allied Industrial Designers, founded in 1959.

When, in 1959, Sir Gordon Russell retired from the Council of Industrial Design,
there was a certain sense that an era had then ended, a link in the long tradition had
been broken. With some questions as to whom, or to what, they owed allegiance,
designers in Britain girded themselves ready for the period of increased
professionalism and aggrandisement, together with a gathering self-doubt, which
lay ahead.

The 1960s

The 1960s was the period in which design in Britain reached its zenith of self-confidence. There was a great deal happening: an increasing public recognition and even, one might say, adulation of designers; a vast expansion in the design profession and also in design education, massively reorganised after the Coldstream Report on Art Education, from 1960 onwards. There was an obvious feeling of the new day dawning and a sudden, reckless, very general enthusiasm, even among the erstwhile caretakers of purism, for the fashionable, ephemeral and zany. British design had never got quite so near vulgarity. Maybe, indeed, the transition proved too rapid, the exuberance too sudden to be easily digested, for by the late 1960s a reaction had set in, leading to a period of painful reappraisal: disquiet among the design student population, which began to question the whole basis of its training; a noticeable edginess in the design profession as new doctrines of design for social usefulness abounded; and, logically in this growing mood of conscientiousness, a reawakened interest in the crafts.

The style of the times was, at its most apparent, a rather knock-out style of ostentatious verve and jollity. Among its attributes was the quality of bigness: large Heal prints, 'Big Circle' carpets and huge Collins & Hayes sofas. The quality of brightness: shining chromed-steel chairs and tables, like those made by Plush Kicker. The quality of jokeyness exemplified by Conran. The cult of carefree youthfulness – 'the hunt for the young' as defined (and encouraged) by *Queen* magazine who in 1967 devoted a whole issue to the Royal College of Art – resulted in a widespread fascination with the images not only of pop and the contemporary drug culture but also with a multiplicity of newly-rediscovered, newly-reworked bygone fashions. Meanwhile, less ostentatious but just as typical, was the large-scale build-up in the 1960s of products designed with an increasing expertise, the design which got Design Awards: such archetypal 1960s prize designs as Kenneth Grange's 'Courier' electric shaver, Robert Heritage's 'Quartet Major' light fittings, the Hille polypropylene chair, the Moulton bicycle, the Adamsez bathroom suite, the famous Friedland chimes. A kind of middle-ground design was seen to be developing. Finally, there was the rising of the Anti-Design movement, identified revealingly by Misha Black in the *Queen* RCA issue, as a post-post-modernism, an idea that the sober, rational and unobtrusive was after all acceptable and even necessary. For as Misha Black pointed out, what use is the eccentric if there is no normal standard with which one can contrast it? His view at the time amounted to an affirmation of the value to society of designers relatively placid in their outlook

176
Tubular steel table and chairs designed by Peter
Wigglesworth and R.V.Exton for Plush Kicker, 1968.
This shiny chromed-steel furniture with its intertwined
curved frame was unmistakably a 'Swinging Sixties'
product. Peter Wigglesworth.

and more plodding in their practice, designers producing objects which 'in their
quiet dignity could provide a domestic and industrial environment in which the gay,
fashionable, nonsensical and exciting would be more enhanced'.

One could say that the 1960s was the period in which design was first recognised
over a wide area. 'Design' was a word which was forever cropping up, used (and
abused) in a profusion of contexts. 'Design' was, at its simplest, the pattern on the
wallpaper. But 'design' was also used for much more complex processes within the
areas of design for engineering, the world of ergonomics and systematic methods in
which the industrial designers of the 1960s were becoming increasingly involved.
For the designer, things were much less straightforward than they had been in the
days when 'good design' seemed mainly a matter of aesthetics: the idea, so current
in the 1950s, that in any visual question the designer's word was final. In the 1960s,
design processes began to be de-mystified. This was the result of the growing

recognition of the relevance of principles of human science, and especially ergonomics, to product design. As John Blake has pointed out in *The Practical Idealists*, his history of Design Research Unit (one of the design practices most obviously attuned to systematic methods), the stress on ergonomics from the early 1960s onwards influenced designing in three main directions. 'First, it emphasised that, in the design of products, the needs of consumers were more important than those of the designer; second, it put forward the, then, rather novel idea that such needs can be determined by scientific means, rather than by guesswork or intuition; and third, it provided a systematic framework for the design activity.' Indeed it can be seen to have influenced a whole new way of thinking about design for industry.

The first articles on systematic methods of designing appeared in *Design* in 1958, and in the next few years the theories of Bruce Archer, J.Christopher Jones and others working in design methodology were widely circulated and discussed. They were not, it must be said, immediately palatable to the design profession: for their basic proposition that design was less a matter of aesthetic intuition than of scientific method, their suggestion that design effectiveness in fact was measurable, undermined the age-old concept that good design is godgiven, a trace of which, of course, has always been a factor in the British tradition of designing. But one outcome of these much-publicised attempts to apply scientific methods of analysis in areas from which they had been noticeably absent, a result of obvious benefit to the design profession, was the way in which design seemed suddenly much more approachable, more comprehensible, more relevant to people who up till then had regarded with suspicion vague assertions of the importance of the visual values. A common language had begun to be discovered. The first conference on systematic methods in designing, held at Imperial College in 1962, a conference which has come to be regarded as something of a milestone in British design history, emphasised how much, in human terms, would be achieved by this breaking down of barriers, the divisions which separated scientist from artist, artist from designer, designer from engineer, engineer from the common man, the user. Design was seen to be the missing link between these sectors. The designer's role had new, important social force.

Design in Britain in the 1960s was much influenced not only by the study of behavioural sciences but also by the techniques of scientific management which had reached Britain from America and which were by now becoming an essential factor in the management of large-scale British industry. Since the War there had been many attempts by the COID to convince industry that design was a top-level management responsibility. At the time of the Festival of Britain – which was, in itself, such a convincing demonstration of the skills of design management the Council recommended – the first tentative Design Management Congress had been held, and there was a much more major one in 1956. The idea that good design is indivisible, that good design should ideally extend to all activities within a company, from the products, packaging and publicity material to the visual standards of the whole working environment (a favourite theme with Gordon Russell), had over the decade been argued with persistence. But it was only in the mid-1960s, undoubtedly encouraged by evidence of new tangible bases for designing, the disciplined approach allied to scientific management, that industry began, at last, to seem convinced. One

177
Flexible chair designed by Nicholas Frewing for Race
Furniture, 1964. Steel mesh seat and back hook into the
beech frame: an ingenious design for home assembly,
typical of that period of knock-down, blow-up furniture.
Alec Gardner-Medwin.

146

178
Polypropylene stacking chair designed by Robin Day for
Hille, 1961. This, perhaps the most instantly recognisable
of post-war British chairs, was the first to have a rigid
shell in polypropylene: a technological innovation of
importance. Hille International.

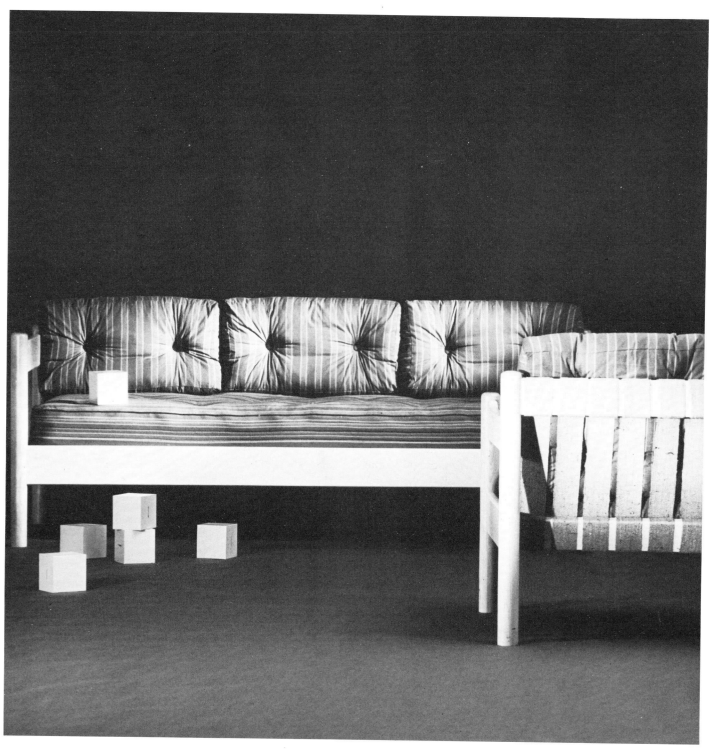

179
179
Bed-sofa with beech frame and striped cotton mattress,
designed by Terence Conran for Conran Furniture,
c.1962. The Conran idiom of the 1960s was basic, solid,
cheerful, much in the tradition of Heal's Cottage
Furniture of the early 1900s. Terence Conran.

180
Children's furniture in corrugated fibreboard, bright red
or royal blue, by Polycell Design Group, 1967. This was
sold packed flat, half furniture, half toy. Polycell.

181
Chromed tubular steel chair with leather seat and back,
designed and made by OMK Design, 1967. A fashionable
1960s chair, without the starkness of Marcel Breuer's
'Wassily' to which it is indebted. OMK Design.
182
Chair in beech designed by Clive Bacon and made by
Design Furnishing Contracts, 1963. One of several
versions of linking/stacking seating developed at this
period for conference halls and churches. The oak chair
by Gordon Russell made originally for Coventry
Cathedral is similar in style. Design Furniture Group.

of the results of this was the emergence of a new kind of designer (or a new kind of
executive) entitled Design Manager, or, at best, Design Director, broadly responsible
for visual liaison within the company: by 1965, the SIA, or the SIAD as it was by then
rechristened, was working towards the setting up of a new category of members to
cover Design Managers, and this became official in 1968. Another sign of the times
was the establishment in 1964 of the Royal Society of Arts Presidential Awards for
Design Management: the first winners, predictably enough, were Heal's, Conran,
Hille, London Transport, Gilbey, Jaeger, firms which had, as the judges put it,
'made a contribution' (a good phrase of the day). With this growing involvement in
management and marketing, the importance of which was stressed with greater
urgency as Britain prepared to join the Common Market, the designers' traditional
role was shifting delicately and, as some saw it, perhaps a little dangerously. The
designer, in this context, was inevitably less of the questioner of accepted values, the
reformer, more of the interpreter of social aspirations, raising very complex
questions of morality indeed.

Reading through the design publications of the period one is very often struck by
the much-increased professionalism of designers. Whereas in the 1950s it was easy
to identify the gentlemanly, British quality of relaxation, a lingering sense of pre-
war hopeful amateurism, by the 1960s the profession had begun to look quite
different, a change of outlook marked, in 1963, by the SIA decision to rename itself
Society of Industrial Artists and *Designers*. In the image-conscious atmosphere of
the mid-1960s, designers were reluctant to present themselves as artists, and Dorothy
Goslett's well-known manual, *Professional Practice for Designers*, published in
1963, became much thumbed. In this mood of general professional expansion,
design offices themselves were getting bigger: in 1967 Design Research Unit had a
staff of 60, including a newly-formed design group specialising in product and
engineering design. Although the design offices were still very much geared to
smaller-scale domestic items – the transistors, the alarm clocks, the food mixers of
that period – some were also well-equipped to design much larger products. Ogle

183
'Form' unit seating designed by Robin Day for Hille in
the late 1950s and winner of a Design Centre Award in
1961. Tania Slowe.

184
Wall storage unit in veneered pine designed by Robert
Heritage for Archie Shine. Robert Heritage trained at
the RCA with Professor R.D.Russell and continued
much of the Russell tradition – that peculiarly English
combination of self-assurance and self-effacement – into
the 1960s. Victoria and Albert Museum.

Design, for instance, were working in the 1960s on such complex projects as the
Ogle Mini, the Electric Taxi, the Raleigh Chopper bicycle, the Reliant Scimitar; and
by 1968, they had set up their own research and product development department.
BIB Design Consultants, formed in 1967, a specifically product design-orientated
group, found that a surprising number, in fact the great majority, of their early
clients came from the area of capital goods.

For this was one direction in which design was moving by the mid-1960s. From
the small beginnings, the early pioneering work in design for the engineering
industries done by the COID in the late 1950s, the possibilities had by now increased
immeasurably. This was a development consistently encouraged by Paul Reilly,
who had succeeded Gordon Russell as Director of the COID in 1960, and it was an
area on which general attention had been focused by the publication, in 1963, of the
report of the government committee, chaired by G.B.R.Feilden, on mechanical-
engineering design. Two years later, a follow-up report, *Industrial and Engineering
Design* (again, produced by a committee chaired by Feilden), was published by the
Federation of British Industries. The report examined in great detail the ways in
which the functions of the designer concerned with the appearance, form and
ergonomics of a product and of the designer concerned with the mechanical and
technical aspects overlapped – 'and, at best, merged'. This clear and concise apologia
for the particular expertise of the industrial designer working in the engineering
industries had, in its period, considerable influence. By the end of the decade, the
number of firms making plant and equipment who used industrial design services
had risen from a negligible figure to a total of some hundreds, and from 1968 the

COID included a Capital Goods section in its annual Design Awards. The establishment, in 1966, of the Engineering Design Centre at Loughborough, and, in 1969, of the Computer-Aided Design Centre in Cambridge, opened out still further prospects for the integration of industrial design.

185
'Thrift' cutlery, stainless steel, designed by David Mellor for the Ministry of Public Buildings and Works, 1965. After commissioning tableware for embassies (see no. 186), the Ministry turned its attention to cutlery for government canteens, hospitals and HM prisons. This led to an economy design in stainless steel in which the customary 11 pieces were reduced to a basic 5-piece setting and the number of production operations were relatively minimal. David Mellor.

186
'Embassy' teapot in silver with black fibre handle,
designed by David Mellor for the Ministry of Public
Buildings and Works, 1963. This teapot was part of an
extensive collection of sterling silver, china and glass
specially commissioned for use in British embassies, an
interesting example of 1960s government conversion to
the 'modern'. The Worshipful Company of Goldsmiths.

187
'Alveston' stainless steel teapot designed by Robert
Welch for Old Hall, 1963. The Worshipful Company of
Goldsmiths.

188
'Beetle' bowl in silver, gilt inside, designed and made by
Gerald Benney, 1962. The Worshipful Company of
Goldsmiths.
189
Stoneware table pottery, designed by Robin Welch in
1968 for production in an individual craft workshop,
an example of small-unit production. Robin Welch.

190
Cast-iron candlesticks with matt black finish, designed
by Robert Welch, 1962. Robert Welch.

154

But where were the industrial designers coming from? One feature of the 1960s,
developing in parallel with the expansion of the design profession, was reorganisation
and substantial upgrading of design education, involving a considerable national
investment. In 1961, as a result of the Coldstream Report on Art Education, which
had recommended the replacement of the National Diploma in Design with a more
liberal, more highly academic system of training for designers, the National Council
for Diplomas in Art and Design was established. The Dip AD was a 'degree-
equivalent' award (not long afterwards replaced by an honours degree proper); and
its implementation, through the decade, led to an enormous enlargement of facilities
and a corresponding increase in teaching staff The Dip AD system covered the
whole spectrum from the Fine Arts to Industrial Design, allowing considerable
freedom to individual colleges, within the general framework of a nationally-
administered system, in the development of their own courses. Some of these were
still relatively craft-based, becoming more, not less, so in the craft renaissance of the
succeeding decade: one thinks, for example, of Sheffield silversmithing or the very
successful craft-based textiles course at Camberwell. But, not surprisingly in this
period of reassessment and expansion, there was also much development in more
scientifically-orientated courses for industrial designers. Whereas before the War,
there had been the smallest handful of quite generalised courses in the large industrial
centres – at Leicester, for instance, and at Birmingham – by the early 1960s the
emphasis on training in industrial design was becoming more widespread, and more
specific. The Industrial Design School at the Royal College of Art, a department

192
'Courier' electric shaver designed by Kenneth Grange for Milward, 1963, and well-known winner of the Duke of Edinburgh's Prize for Elegant Design. Kenneth Grange.

which developed from the Wood, Metal and Plastics School of the early years of the RCA revival, had a notably productive period in the 1960s under Misha Black, then the Professor, and Frank Height; and it was during this regime that the Industrial Design Research Unit, directed by Bruce Archer, was first established in 1961.

Interestingly enough, although this was a period for such extensive schemes and super-sized design commissions (*Design* magazine, at the time, seemed to be full of pictures of Design Award-winning earth-moving equipment), it was also a time when the climate for more experimental and esoteric enterprises had never seemed more right. OMK Design was a typical example: a small, experimental and remarkably successful furniture-manufacturing company founded in 1966 by three ex-students of the furniture department of the Central School, Jurek Olejnik, Bryan Morrison and Rodney Kinsman, hence OMK. Osborne-Little Wallpapers began in 1968, again a very small-scale, individual operation which continued and expanded through the 1970s. The tenor of the times, as one sees it from so many contemporary publications on design, was not only one of systematic methods and level-headed planning, but also quite the opposite: the 1960s also had an extreme naïve self-confidence, a touching faith in visual flair and intuition, which was, of course, being boosted – as it had, indeed, been earlier, back in the 1880s – by a supporting body of design-conscious consumers, sophisticated people on the track of special objects with which to enhance the reputation of their life-style. This was much to the advantage not only of the older-established design-minded shops like Heal's and Dunn's of Bromley, but also of the newly-modernised large stores, of which Woollands, Knightsbridge, was the supreme example. There was a sudden spate of new, small, personal design shops, some of which, in fact, were being opened by designers in a new role (or a role only new since William Morris) of simultaneous designer, manufacturer and shopkeeper. One of these was Terence Conran, who opened the first Habitat in Fulham Road, South Kensington, in 1964.

It is difficult, perhaps, for those who never knew it to understand fully the impact of that Habitat. It was so very much a symbol of that period, an expression of the youth cult, much attuned to swinging Chelsea, a fascinating mixture of the amateur and knowing, the naïve and the cynical, the sensitive and brash. The inordinate success of Mary Quant's Bazaar in Knightsbridge, which Conran had designed in 1963, encouraged Terence Conran to open Habitat, a 'shop for switched-on people', as his press release described it. And really Habitat and Bazaar were very similar; they serviced (and indeed half-created) the same life-style. What more perfect 1960s vision, for worldly London people, than sitting on a Conran sofa dressed in clothes by Quant? Besides the furniture, which was made at Conran's factory in Thetford, one of the *raisons d'être* of the first Habitat, the shop also sold lighting, fabrics, china, glass and kitchenware, household equipment immaculately chosen but displayed with a brilliantly-calculated randomness. The overall image was sophisticated peasant, for although the individual objects were quite purist, sound enough to have passed muster with the early DIA, the general atmosphere was cheery, rather homely, and this was very much a part of its success. The point was that 'good design', as it had been put over for so many years by the official propagandists and the private devotees, had, to many people, seemed a little daunting: somehow it had a certain element of grimness. But Conran, almost by

193
Traffic signal system designed by David Mellor with the
Ministry of Transport, installed nationally from 1969.
As a result of the Worboys Report, the traffic signal
system was overhauled and rationalised: the optical
system was intensified, and plastics or plastics-coated
materials were introduced to minimise maintenance
costs. Plessey Controls.

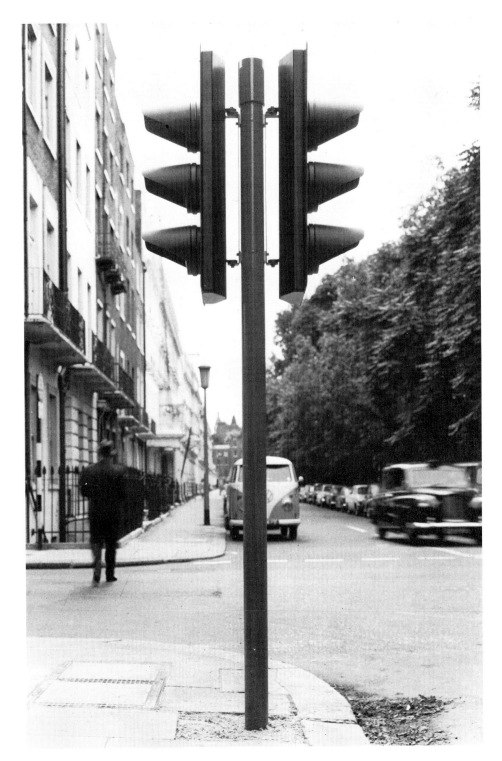

194
Moulton bicycle designed by Alex Moulton and
manufactured by Moulton Bicycles, 1964. A radical
rethinking of bicycle design, superbly well engineered.
Moulton Bicycles.

195
Garden shears with beech handles, designed by Hulme
Chadwick for Wilkinson Sword, 1964. Victoria and
Albert Museum.
196
'Barbican' hand-rinse basin designed by Chamberlin,
Powell and Bon with Twyfords, 1966. Victoria and
Albert Museum.

some sleight of hand, succeeded in gaining acceptance from a fairly general public
for principles the experts had been trying to put over for so long so relatively
ineffectively: good design could, at last, be seen to be accessible; good design could
even be proved to be amusing. And even if, as Habitat succeeded Habitat (for by
1968, four new stores had opened), the idea, inevitably maybe, lost its freshness, its
totally convincing sense of personal vision, it was still one of the 1960s most
remarkable phenomena and set a whole new standard of retailing in Britain.

The pursuit of individuality, which has been a constantly recurring theme within
design in Britain, was clearly on the increase from the mid-1960s onwards. Perhaps
this should be seen as a necessary safety valve in case the systematic methods grew
oppressive, an inbuilt corrective against encroaching dullness. In this decade, for
instance, there was a quite remarkable, and in many ways completely unexpected,
revival of the craft of silversmithing. This can be attributed partly to the influence
of Robert Goodden, a notably effective RCA Professor of Jewellery and
Silversmithing, partly to the energetic practical support of Graham Hughes, the Art

197
Door bells, chimes and buzzers, designed by Norman Stevenson for Friedland, early 1960s. A determined attempt to impose 'sixties-modern' styling on the traditional door-chimes of English bourgeois life, which, deservedly, won a Design Centre Award in 1964. Friedland.

198
Pay-on-answer coin box, designed by Douglas Scott with the GPO, c.1960. British Post Office.

199
'Quartet Major' light fittings designed by Robert
Heritage for Rotaflex, 1964. Victoria and Albert
Museum.
200
'Merlin' electric alarm-clock, designed by Robert Welch
for Westclox, 1964. Robert Welch.

201
'Brownie Vecta' camera designed by Kenneth Grange
for Kodak, 1964. The vertical design was based on the
premise that most domestic photographs consist of one
or two human figures in the standing position. Kenneth
Grange.

161

Director of the Worshipful Company of Goldsmiths. Several dozen new workshops were set up in this period, some – like Gerald Benney's and Louis Osman's – concentrating on special commissions; others – like Robert Welch's and David Mellor's – combining craft silversmithing with industrial design. This was characteristic 1960s thinking. In this period, as well, there were the beginnings of a strong new movement in craft pottery, together with a similar new interest in weaving, developments signalled by the exhibition in the 1960s of weaving by Collingwood and pottery by Coper at the Victoria and Albert Museum, the first time that the Museum showed the work of living craftsmen and the start of a new policy of contemporary exhibitions and commissions. Another memorable exhibition, held at the Design Centre in 1965, was 'Hand and Machine' which emphasised the traditional overlap of craft and mass production within design in Britain.

Seen from the 1980s, these were halcyon days indeed. But maybe the excitement was too frenzied to be lasting. Although the decade had been in many ways so fruitful, as well as so eventful, for the design profession, the 1960s did not end as well as they began. They ended on a note of acrimony and anxiety. 'Will the designer', asked Bruce Archer in an article on design management in *Design* in 1969, 'be fit to face the world of the 70s? Can he adapt himself to the highly professional, multi-disciplinary team: to the vertical integration of industrial innovation? Is he willing and able to provide the link – the calculable link – between the absolute value, marginal value, price, premium and cost without losing control of those intangible, cultural values of which he must remain the guardian?' This was just the kind of question, asked with increasing earnestness, destined to divide designers into sheep and goats, wise and foolish virgins; for though some designers were fit, indeed quite eager, others were noticeably reluctant to face a future full of costs and premiums, not to menion values absolute and marginal. Somehow the prospects seemed a little unalluring, even maybe rather dubious. Questions of designers' professional morality were, by the late 1960s, causing noticeable angst, a situation exacerbated by the student troubles of 1968, and with the approach of the 1970s, a period of remarkable design polarisation, the designers who resisted the whole concept of the vertical integration of industrial innovation (together with those who simply did not understand it), could be detected digging themselves in for the long forthcoming winter of Alternative Design.

The 1970s

The 1970s was a period of extremes within design in Britain. A period of new professionalism for designers, as technological advances in industry demanded corresponding expertise in the design profession, together with a newly-realistic working knowledge of the managerial skills of designing for a market. And also, surprisingly and simultaneously, a time for the renaissance of that amateur approach, that apparently spontaneous, almost off-hand creativity, at which, from time to time, the British are so brilliant. The craft revival movement, which involved the setting up of many dozens of new, individual, often experimental workshops, had been stimulated greatly by the establishment of the government-financed Crafts Advisory Committee (later the Crafts Council); and in this period, the small craft workshops were a source of considerable vitality and optimism. Meanwhile, the mood of intensified awareness of their social responsibilities, a major preoccupation of designers in the conscience-stricken 1960s, continued through the 1970s, the memorable slogans of the period being 'Nearness to Need' and 'Design for the Real World'.

The styles of the time had never seemed such poles apart as they were in the 1970s, so totally divided between the self-effacing and the self-expressive. The Anti-Design tendencies defined by Misha Black back in the mid-1960s had come into their own with the emergent new technology; design, when applied to microprocessor technology, was, it seemed, reduced to a succession of black boxes. Design in the 1970s had, to say the very least, a certain sameness. This was the era for design so unobtrusive it was almost non-existent, the triumph of anonymity. Or so it seemed. For Anti-Design, in the 1970s, was balanced by a concurrent movement of great individuality in which, interestingly enough, some of the themes of the early Arts and Crafts movement were often much in evidence. There was the new mania for perfection of technique, exemplified by John Makepeace's furniture and Gerald Benney's silver. New interest in reworking the vernacular tradition, as in the pottery of Michael Casson, John Leach and Richard Batterham; the rag rugs of John Hinchcliffe. A fresh preoccupation with allusiveness and narrative, as shown by the work of Michael Lloyd in silver: his bowls with trees and moons and grass and corn are right in the tradition of Arts and Crafts symbolic. There has been, in the past decade, a noticeable zest for sheer decorative qualities, the qualities which, in a sense, had been denied to designers in Britain through many long years of the puritan aesthetic. One also finds, in some of the craftwork of the 1970s, a growing sense of double entendre, a subtle wit.

The Crafts Advisory Committee began work in 1971. This was the first time that the importance of the work of British craftsmen, their role in the whole cultural pattern of the country, had really been recognised by central government. The Committee was set up by Lord Eccles, Paymaster General and Minister responsible for the Arts, under the wing of the Council of Industrial Design whose Director, Sir Paul Reilly, had for some years felt the need to coordinate the activities of the different (and often divergent) craft societies by forming a more powerful and far-sighted central body. The Committee's main concern, from its inception, was with the work of 'artist-craftsmen', as its early brief defined them: craftsmen whose work, although often rooted in traditional techniques, has an aim which extends beyond the reproduction of past styles and methods. In other words, its bias was very much towards the creative crafts, and its chief executive, later its Director, was Victor Margrie, himself a well-known potter. Its task was seen as a dual one:

202
Chair in elm designed and made by Richard La Trobe-Bateman, 1977. A version of the traditional smoker's chair, showing the new mood of nostalgic innovation in the craft revival furniture of the 1970s. Richard La Trobe-Bateman.

203
Ebony chair designed by John Makepeace and made by
Andrew Whately in Makepeace's workshops at Parnham,
1978. The woven seat and back are nickel silver, and the
chair has both the finesse and the touch of eccentricity
typical of Makepeace's most recent work. Private
collection.

promotional, focusing public attention on the work of modern artist-craftsmen;
and practical, in giving grants to new craft workshops, helping to finance craft-
workshop training, and supporting regional craft activities. Its first major exhibition,
'The Craftsman's Art' held in 1973 at the Victoria and Albert Museum, was an
extraordinary public success; *Crafts* magazine was started that same year; a London
exhibition gallery was opened and an index of craftsmen began to be built up.
Through active, one might almost say intrepid, attempts to bring the public face to
face with artist-craftsmen, culminating in the sponsoring of nationwide tours called
'Meet the Craftsmen', the work of the CAC enormously intensified public awareness
of who craftsmen are and what they can contribute. By 1979, by which time it had
become an independent body, redesignated the Crafts Council, its *raison d'être* was
no longer in question, with a grant which had increased from the £178,000 of its
first year of operation to £1,148,000 for 1978–9.

And yet, for all the success of the Crafts Council in stimulating British craft
activity, it has to be remembered that the seeds were there already. The basic
impulse for the widespread craft revival came not from the Crafts Council but
directly from the craftsmen. The Crafts Council activities to some extent were
simply a reflection of the ideas and the interests which had been steadily
accumulating in the 1960s and which were, in themselves, a development of even
older attitudes towards design and making. These went back, in fact, as far as the
ideas of William Morris and the principle of making things not mainly to make
money but because these are the things which you, quite simply, want to make.

206
Desk from the 'Ash Occasional' range designed by
Dinah Casson for Remploy Furniture, 1979. A design
which demonstrates convincingly a continuity of attitude
to furniture from Gimson to Russell to Heritage and
Carter and on to the RCA designers of the 1970s.
Remploy.

207
Cabinet in sycamore, designed and made by John
Coleman, then a final-year student at the Royal College
of Art, 1979. John Coleman.
208 (*right*)
'Tipster' chair designed by Robert Heritage and Roger
Webb for Race Furniture, 1979. The chair both stacks
and links and has a tip-up seat. Race Furniture.

209 (*opposite*)
'Octave' seating designed by Ronald Carter for Collins & Hayes, 1968. An early version of a concept which became very general in the 1970s: the free-form seating unit, the antithesis of the three-piece suite. Collins & Hayes.

The craft revival of the early 1970s was well within the British tradition of idealism. Though it lacked the element of selflessness, the broadly humanistic outlook of the Arts and Crafts movement of the end of the last century, it showed a similar concern with, and distaste for, the materialist structure of contemporary life: it was, in the same way, a very obvious protest movement against the prevailing attitudes to working and standards of environment. It was, once again, a reassertion of individuality, of personal creativity, in a very complex industrial society. It evinced a comparable longing to get back to what were seen as the real and lasting values, which often involved setting up a workshop in the country; for in the 1970s, as in the 1890s, the real lasting values almost always meant rurality. The modern craft revival has been very much in tune with the progressive preoccupations of its time; linked through to the good lifers, natural foods and natural fibres, the drinkers of real ale and the makers of real bread. It can also, perhaps, be seen as the corollary of rather more specific discontents and disenchantments with current tendencies in the design profession, a rejection of the concept of design-for-marketing, the designer as the tool of the materialist society. The craftsmen in a sense set up an opposition faction. This was, of course, the camp which appealed most to many students who embraced the craft revival with a good deal too much fervour. From the design-orientated ideals of the 1950s, when students' main aim was to go out and work in industry, there had now been a total *volte-face* and the dream of the preponderance of students in the 1970s was to set up a craft workshop. In the end the craft revival got a little out of hand.

What it did, which was important, was to redirect attention back to the skills of making. These had partly been forgotten in the early post-war period when emphasis in education was becoming more highly academic: heady days of design-for-industry when the crafts, in most progressive circles, were taboo. In 1977, a sign of the new climate of opinion, the John Makepeace School for Craftsmen in Wood was opened, funded by the non-profit-making Parnham Trust. This school, run alongside John Makepeace's own furniture workshops at Parnham House in Dorset, was set up to train more craftsmen to open more craft workshops: a project unimaginable fifteen years before.

Out of the craft revival, too, came a new interest by designers in involving themselves in actual methods of production. The craft revival, joined with the attractions of the small-is-beautiful philosophy, stimulated the move towards small-unit production. This had many permutations. The small-batch-producing craftsman with one or two assistants, as, for instance, John Leach, making a repeatable standard range of pottery, employing entirely hand-production methods. The craftsman such as Robin Welch, the Suffolk potter, adapting industrial techniques for standardised production in what was still essentially a craft workshop. The designer-manufacturer like David Mellor who in 1973 set up his own cutlery factory in Sheffield, a production unit very highly mechanised yet small enough in scale for freedom of manœuvre, in which the designer would be able to control not only the details of each product but also the layout of the factory and the design of the production machinery. The 1970s were notable for the success of designers, such as Peter Simpson at Bute Fabrics, Frank Thrower at Dartington Glass, in bridging the gap, in small-to-medium size firms, between sales and production. Here, looming

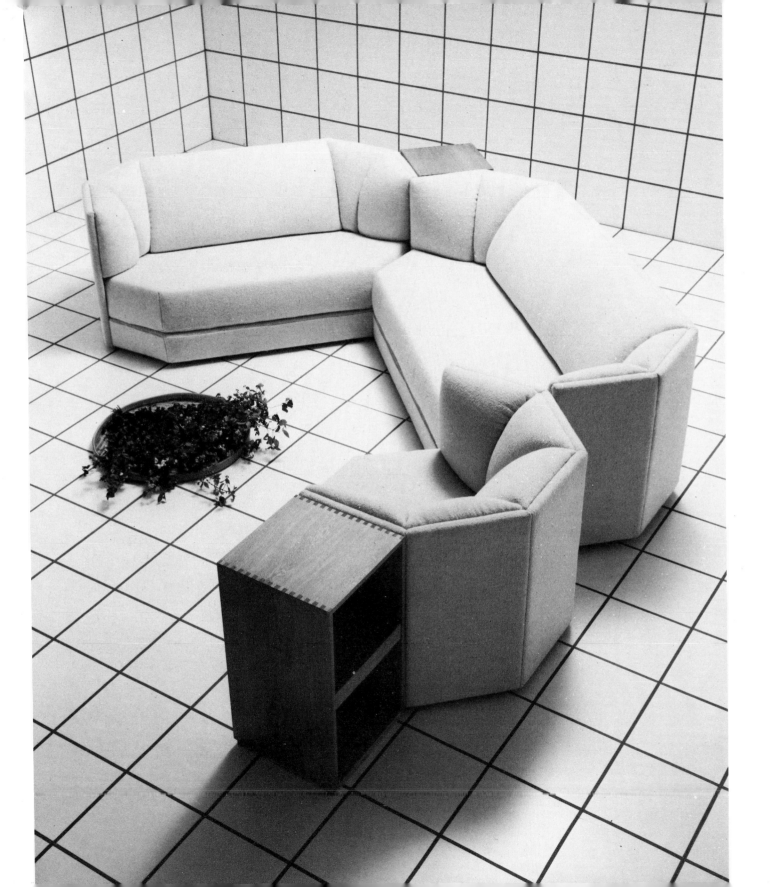

'Omstack' chair with pressed steel seat and back, designed by Rodney Kinsman for OMK, 1970. OMK Design.

large, was the missing technician whose absence John Gloag, long ago, had so lamented. The pattern of designer-director, involved in all stages of design, from conception to final production and marketing, could be seen continuing into the 1980s with the small-unit furniture firm Peter Miles Furniture, set up in 1980 at Wirksworth in Derbyshire by Peter Miles and Ronald Carter RDI.

The 1970s became a very specialist decade. Gone were the days of the small all-purpose offices; going, too, was the concept of the versatile designer, central to the

211
'Chinese Ivory' cutlery, stainless steel with acetal resin handles, designed and manufactured by David Mellor, 1977. Metal parts are blanked out of flat strip steel, and this gives the design its distinctive visual character. David Mellor.

British tradition since the 1930s, the idea of the designer who could turn his hand to anything, design on any scale, from a machine tool to a teacup. Now, in a way ironically, since design horizons had widened so immeasurably in the post-war period, design practice had itself become more narrow, the areas of influence much tighter, more specific. This change was reflected by a greatly altered emphasis in the work of the Council of Industrial Design which in 1972 became the Design Council, having been invited by the government (as its 1972–3 Report explains it) 'to pursue

174

212
Silver bowl, raised by Peter Musgrove, engraved by
Malcolm Appleby, 1975. The craft silver of the 1970s
became much freer in its decoration, showing new
preoccupation with surface patterning and reawakened
interest in symbolic forms. Crafts Council collection.
213
Large stoneware storage jar by Peter Starkey, 1975. The
salt-glaze, the combed decoration, the sheer usefulness
of this jar would place it well within the English country
potters' functional tradition; yet it has a wittiness, a
visual sophistication, which makes it very much a pot of
the mid-1970s, an excellent example of Peter Starkey's
work. W.A.Ismay.
214
Handmade glass, small-batch production, designed and
made by Simon Pearce, 1975. Simon Pearce.
215
Small pots in white bone china with relief decoration, by
Jacqueline Poncelet, 1975. Crafts Council collection.

216
'Concept' tea-set in vitrified earthenware, designed by
Martin Hunt for Hornsea Pottery, 1977, and winner –
with David Mellor's 'Chinese Ivory', no. 211 – of a
Design Award in that same year. Hornsea Pottery.

217
Cast-iron cooking pots with black enamelled finish,
designed by Robert Welch, 1970. Robert Welch.

175

218
'SM2000' direct-drive record turntable, part of a range of high-performance hi-fi equipment designed by PA Design Unit for Strathearn Audio, 1975. PA Technology and Science Centre.

219
Secateurs designed by DCA Design Consultants for Stanley Garden Tools, mid-1970s. Stanley Tools.

its campaigns beyond the boundaries of industrial design and graphic design even more rigorously than before into the vastly more powerful and complex realms of engineering'. In the fifteen years or so since its first tentative campaigns for design within the engineering industries, the Council's own approach had been becoming more sophisticated and professional. Where once the stress had been on the obvious 'design' qualities, aesthetic appearance and ergonomics, the Council had moved on to campaign for what it termed as total excellence: to consider not only ergonomics and appearance but also innovation, function, economy and efficiency in manufacture and use.

The change in general outlook in the 1970s, as well as the expansion in the work of the Design Council, is illustrated nicely by a quick comparison of the first group of Design Centre Awards, given in 1957, with the Design Awards of twenty years later. Both, in their way, are vintage collections. But whereas the early awards are

220
'Executive' calculator designed and manufactured by Sinclair Radionics, 1972. Victoria and Albert Museum.
221
'Powerflood' floodlamp system designed by Robert Heritage for Concord Lighting, 1971. Concord Lighting International.

222
Push-Button Telephone, one of a range designed by DCA Design Consultants for British Telecom, 1979.

223
Fire-engine cab developed by Ogle Design with Dennis Motors, 1978. Dennis Motors.

224
'Boss Mark III' front-loading fork lift truck, designed by London & Upjohn with Lancer Boss design team and manufactured by Lancer Boss; winner of Capital Goods Design Award in 1970. Lancer Boss.

225
Truck-mounted hydraulic telescopic Crane 725 CM, designed by D.Hassall and Cosmos design team for Cosmos Crane Co., 1976. This crane was intended for high-speed lifting and placing of loads, with rapid transit between work sites. The design shows great attention to practical detail, including exceptional provision for the comfort of the driver, minimising the dangers of operator fatigue. Cosmos Crane Co.

all domestic, from the Rotaflex lampshades to the Strawberry Hill china, the 1977 Awards are much more varied, many of them much more technical, immensely further reaching, far beyond the ken of the ordinary housewife who so preoccupied those early design panels. The 1977 Awards came in five categories. Consumer and Contract Goods, extending from digital clocks and pocket calculators to the Topper Sailing Dinghy; the pottery tea-set and the stainless steel cutlery seemed almost to be pieces from a long-forgotten era. Awards were given to Engineering Products: spectrophotometers, sidelift trucks and telescopic boom cranes. Awards were also given to Engineering Components, such products as high-performance gear pumps and powered cable reels. The fourth category was the British Motor Vehicle Industry. The fifth for Medical Equipment. Nowhere was the change of emphasis so marked as in this last highly technical, professional and specialist category in which the awards ranged from the Charnley-Howorth Sterile Operating Unit and the Wilj Gamma-Counting system to a set of particularly well-designed false teeth.

'Industrial design is now fifty years on', as Frank Height so truly commented in 1977, in his RCA Professorial Address, 'and has grown out of its heroic period'. By the 1970s, the heroes, the individual stars of the design world, were either dead and buried or else keeping a low profile. In industrial design, the scene was now too complex for old-style atelier-based British designing, and in training designers for the engineering industries the stress was now on teamwork, on specific expertise. New professionalism in attitudes to training of designers in the country as a whole, in the design departments of many Polytechnics, as well as at the RCA, became apparent, and moves were being made to integrate the training of industrial and engineering designers. In 1980, mainly at the instigation of Professor Frank Height, a course in industrial design engineering was introduced, run jointly by the RCA and Imperial College of Science and Technology, for graduate engineers and scientists; at the same time, collaboration had begun between the RCA and Cranfield Institute of Technology, including the establishment of two related Fellowships, one based at the RCA and one at Cranfield, directed to Computer-Aided Design.

Design offices enlarged and equipped themselves to tackle more specialist projects. Bill Moggridge Associates, for instance, a practice founded in 1969, has specialised increasingly in microelectronics, in office technology, telecommunications, scientific and engineering equipment, and by 1980 had set up a second unit in the Silicon Valley area, near San Francisco. Allied Industrial Designers, established by James Pilditch in 1959, now the largest design consultancy in Britain with a staff of 100, has pursued an energetic marketing-directed policy. In 1980, the year in which AID became a public company, the first design consultancy in Britain to go public, they acquired two further companies: Business Decisions Ltd, a market-research company; and DVW Microelectronics Ltd, a firm which designs and develops microprocessor-based products and processes. James Pilditch's reasoning in acquiring DVW was that since the product designers in his office had already been designing the 'outer casing' for a number of electronic products, and since the software firm had designed a lot of interior mechanisms, it made sense to offer a combined service. Besides, he added, AID had a good 'innovations' group, helping firms to develop new products, and it was obviously impossible to be effective in that particular aspect of designing without knowing what microelectronics were about.

226
High-Speed Diesel Train developed by British Rail and
first put into service in 1975. Kenneth Grange of
Pentagram was design consultant for the power cab, and
working to a brief of extraordinary complexity, arrived
at a solution which is admirably British, functional and
elegant, a design of which Frank Pick would surely have
approved. British Railways Board.

227
'Mini-Variset' cloakroom system designed by Kenneth
Grange for A.J.Binns, 1978. Extruded aluminium rail
with grey nylon hooks and straps. A.J.Binns.

228
Monitor Terminal designed by Kenneth Grange for
Reuters, 1980. The system provides information for the
money market: the cabinet houses a 9-inch screen data
terminal; the alpha-numeric control keyboard is used
remotely. Reuters.

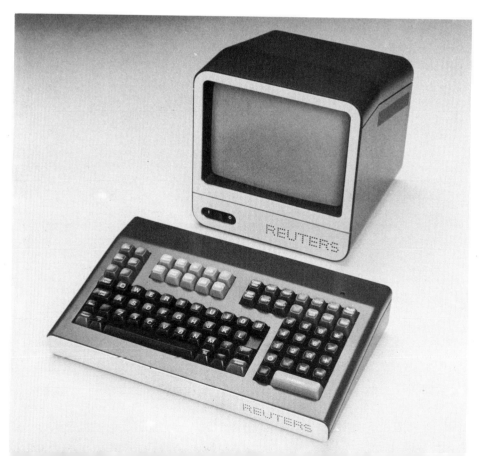

229

'Witney' sideboard in stained mahogany, designed by Ronald Carter for Peter Miles Furniture. An excellent example of the neo-Arts and Crafts style of the early 1980s, superbly well detailed and immaculately made. Peter Miles Furniture.

As the 1970s progressed, the design world was becoming a very different place, more competitive, more thrusting, more obviously allied to the marketing and advertising agencies than at any previous period in British design history. The national economic crisis, joined with the problems of a world recession, had the effect of toughening the design profession, with lip-service being paid rather more to marketing than art. One effect of the recession in Britain was to propel British design firms to look for work abroad. In this, they were remarkably successful. By 1980, Pentagram Design had opened an office in New York: thirty to forty per cent of its design work was being done for clients outside Britain. BIB Design Group, a specialist product design practice was, again, by 1980, working for a forty per cent foreign clientele, including four Japanese companies. Conran Associates, with an office in Paris, were also doing a great deal of work abroad, especially in shop design. Their policy, as propounded by John Stephenson, Managing Director, in a statement to *The Times*, was straightforwardly aggressive. The Conran group, he said, was 'as much run by businessmen as designers'. Its philosophy was 'making money', a policy so unashamedly materialistic as to bring British design almost back to where it started.

230
Battery whisk, a low-cost hand-held food mixer designed
by Kenneth Grange for Kenwood Manufacturing Co.,
1975. Kenneth Grange.
231
'Parker 25' pen range, designed by Kenneth Grange for
the Parker Pen Co., 1975. Kenneth Grange.

In the 1970s, Conran won commissions for three fairly similar ranges of plastics
kitchenware for three different clients, Boots/Timothy Whites, Marks & Spencer
and Woolworths: a considerable achievement both in terms of skilful business and
in terms of bringing good design to the mass markets. But in terms of human need?
Well, that was surely a rather different question, another kind of argument. It was
interesting how, as the 1970s developed, attitudes and aims among professional
designers became more and more divergent. What were their true objectives? What
was good design about? The large businesslike consultancies had one idea: that
good design was, simply, commercially effective. But a much more earnest view, the
more traditional belief that the best design was socially beneficial, that designers
had community responsibilities, had many strong adherents. This was the great age
of ecological awareness, and as the Design Council Annual Report for 1976–7
pointed out, in the new and frugal mood of conservationism, the designers' built-in
talents were particularly relevant: 'Seldom can the hallowed principles of good
design, whether expressed as economy of means or intelligence made visible, have
been more in tune with the times than in the mid-nineteen seventies.' It was, after
all, the metier of the designer, both by training and by instinct, to search out the
simplest, most economical solution to any problem; many designers, the Report
suggested, 'may even welcome the new restrictions as a recall to sober, functional,
socially valid yardsticks'.

Certainly, through the 1970s, the number of socially valid design activities grew
rapidly. The SIAD, for instance, set up an Alternative Design Group; the DIA

inaugurated a series of Melchett Awards, annual prizes for research into socially-responsible design. The handbook of the movement was, of course, Victor Papanek's *Design for the Real World*, and its focal event the 'Design for Need' symposium and exhibition held at the RCA in 1976. As a result of this conference, an intense new awareness of the potential social implications of designers' work developed. This was particularly strong in the design schools. The consciousness that the work of the designer had its hazards, in terms of consumption of resources and also possible harmful side-effects, was balanced by the perception that design could be a positive force for the improvement of conditions among the aged, the infirm, the socially disadvantaged, all areas which up till then had suffered from neglect. The needs of the Third World began to be considered, and in 1977 the RCA established a specialised section within its School of Industrial Design for studies in Resources, Environment, Aid and Development (generally known, conveniently, as READ).

It is perhaps significant that, through this pursuit of social validity, design to some extent rediscovered its identity. The repeated emphasis on the moral issues of industrial design had, by the end of the decade, reinstated the designer in the role of reconciler, the link-figure, the agent through whom the enormous possibilities of modern technology took on a comprehensible, humanitarian form. In the late 1970s, the crucial importance of design-awareness in society was being argued very plausibly on many different levels. Dr Patrick Nuttgens was putting the case forward for a new and much more practical approach to higher education, a greater concentration on 'the world of doing and making'. Dr Bruce Archer was theorising cogently about the need to recognise an academic discipline besides the traditional sciences and humanities: the missing discipline was seen to be designing. And, in the persuasive and powerful report on *Design Education at Secondary Level*, published by the Design Council in 1980, Professor David Keith-Lucas, Chairman of the working party, emphasised the gap in national educational policy at a more fundamental stage. 'If education', he wrote, 'is concerned with trying to fit children to play a full part in the adult life of tomorrow, there can be few more important educational experiences for the children than to grapple with the sort of problems they will meet as adults – problems of the environment, of man-made things and how they can be improved, of the quality of living – or, in other words, "design" in all its forms.'

Into the 1980s

Over the past century enormous energy and indeed expertise have been directed towards the improvement of national design standards; or, to put it more accurately, towards bringing national standards into line with what the design cognoscenti recommended. The belief that such a revolution in taste was not only feasible on a national scale but also actually socially beneficial dominated the campaigns of the succession of reform groups: the late nineteenth-century Arts and Crafts societies and the short-lived but vociferous National Association for the Advancement of Art and its Application to Industry; the Design and Industries Association in the period between the Wars; the Pick Council in the 1930s. This was the thinking, optimistic and paternal, behind the stepping up of the campaign for good design in the early post-war period: the expansion of the Council of Industrial Design; the reorganisation of the Royal College of Art; and later, in the 1960s, the considerable enlargement and upgrading of the whole national network for the training of designers, by then mainly within the large-scale Polytechnic system.

The national design establishment is now extensive. By 1980, the Design Council had expanded from its original ten staff in 1945 to around 230; its grant had increased from £550,000 in 1970 to £2,811,000 in 1980. The Crafts Council received a further £1m. Design education had enlarged dramatically: the number of Polytechnics and Colleges approved by the Council for National Academic Awards for degree courses in 3-Dimensional Design had risen from 22 in 1970 to 31 in 1980; the equivalent figures for Fashion and Textiles courses were 16 in 1970, 23 in 1980. In 1980 (the most recent year for which figures are available) CNAA degrees were awarded to 609 3-Dimensional Design students, 581 students of Fashion and Textiles, and 93 students in the relatively new, but fast-growing, area of History of Art and Design. With so many resources directed towards training, the design profession has shown signs of an explosion. Membership of the Society of Industrial Artists and Designers had risen from the ten or so of 1930 to 3,500 in 1970 to 6,500 in 1980; and the total is still multiplying rapidly.

The efforts, the resources, the build-up of activity in British design has been enormously impressive; the idea has been pursued with more energy in Britain than in any other country. But what of the results? Is Britain, as it should be, by now design world leader? If one answers truthfully, one has to answer no. The fact is, and in the 1980s it began to be admitted, that British design, compared with that of other nations such as Italy, Japan and Germany, lacks sophistication. What is more, the gulf between the standards of accepted taste among the pundits and the national aesthetic as one sees it in the High Streets has never seemed so obvious, so totally unbridgeable. Good design is still, just as it appeared at the time of Pevsner's 1937 national survey, an almost wholly middle-class preserve: the upper class ignores it; the working man rejects it. Indeed, perhaps the gap seems even greater than it was, for there were signs in the 'contemporary' era, the period surrounding the Festival of Britain, of a growth of understanding, almost a *rapprochement*, between the purists and the taste of the mass market. But those days of hope are over and the purists now left stranded, the tucket sounding faintly. There is only Habitat.

The early 1980s have proved an anxious period of stock-taking and soul-searching. The death of Gordon Russell, who embodied a whole movement in British design history, from Arts and Crafts to modern; the retirement of the close-knit group of RCA Professors who had been a powerful influence since the days of Robin Darwin; the break-up of the old hierarchies; the erosion of old certainties in British design attitudes: all this has contributed to a vague sense of dislocation in the design profession. There are also the problems and frustrations of the current economic situation, within which there seems so little experimental leeway. A long-drawn-out period of financial retrenchment is inevitably hard for those whose job is innovation. But this is surely only half the explanation: there has been a good deal more to it than that.

Some of the unease of designers in the 1980s has arisen from the feeling, a gradually growing suspicion, that their energies have tended to be misdirected. Has the moral emphasis in British design tradition, a deep-rooted distrust of capitalist practice which goes back as far as Ruskin and Morris, together with a dilettante attitude to marketing, resulted in designers, especially designers in the consumer industries, failing to carry ideas through with clear conviction? 'Many talented designers', said Terence Conran sternly in autumn 1980, 'have not achieved success for themselves, or their clients, because they have not studied the market properly before they conceived their designs, or followed the product through from the manufacturer to the consumer, checking that at every stage the design is properly presented. So many designers still believe that if form follows function and the product is efficiently manufactured, then their job has been well done.' There were few to disagree with him. Design ideals have sharpened since the early 1950s, and by the 1980s it is obvious to designers that the decent job, plain and simple, is not enough. It has become clear that more research is needed into product innovation and marketing, and in 1981 Frank Height, Professor of Industrial Design at the RCA, was strenuously advocating the establishment of an advanced institute of design, sponsored by both government and industry, to determine the directions which new design should take.

Artistic uncertainties have also proved disorientating to the designers of the early 1980s. The immense technological advances of the past decade, the phenomenon described by Frank Height as 'the triumph of invisible technology', has left the designer, whose professionalism is based on an essentially visual interpretation of the physical world, in an understandable state of disarray. The ground, in a sense, has been shifted from beneath him. The old aesthetic theories seem to have lost their relevance. The form-follows-function idea has become redundant when the actual mechanism of the product is in some cases so complex as to be beyond the designer's comprehension in any but the very broadest terms. The designers of microelectronics products have, for instance, in some ways a more demanding task than designers of more traditional artefacts because here the design solution is open-ended. Designers, in this context, can do anything they choose to. They can (the solution most in favour in the 1970s) put the components neatly into little boxes, giving an appearance of functional efficiency, although in fact the form is not particularly relevant to what goes on inside it. Or, an approach now becoming much more fashionable, the designer can by-pass a merely functional appearance and shape the object for the emotional satisfaction, or indeed the sheer amusement, of the customer.

The 1980s show signs of being the decade in which form-follows-function changes very subtly, but in fact quite radically, to form-expresses-function. We are back to the yearning for symbolism; emotional overtones; mystery and myth; all of which is possible, indeed extremely tempting, in designing in relation to the new technology. Here, again, is the designer in the role of the interpreter, designer as the form-giver to human understanding. An exhibit in the 1981 Degree Shows at the RCA was a paramount example of the new poetic tendencies. This was a convector heater encased not, as it would have been in years gone by, in smart grey unobtrusive squared-off metal sheeting, but taking the free form of a convector-heater-sculpture expressing, logically enough, a puff of wind.

British design books and exhibition catalogues

Since the publication of Anthony Coulson's massively informative *Bibliography of Design in Britain 1851–1970* (London, Design Council, 1979), any further attempt to compile a comprehensive book list would be superfluous. For those who need to find it, everything is there.

This list is therefore more of a personal selection of books I have found particularly useful or illuminating. Some are the obvious, essential, major studies of the design and the designers of this period. Others are obscurer, but have some special quality of originality or authenticity which, in my opinion, makes them worthwhile hunting out.

The same is broadly true of the exhibition catalogues. These, I think, can be especially informative. The contemporary catalogues – say, from 'Britain Can Make It', and the Festival of Britain – have an extraordinary immediacy even now. The retrospective catalogues, of whatever period, give a very valuable insight into contemporary ratings: how particular designers or movements in design seemed to the cognoscenti of the time. I have of course included the seminal exhibitions, those – such as 'Victorian and Edwardian Decorative Arts' at the Victoria and Albert Museum in 1952 – which influenced the attitude of its whole generation. But I have also selected from the increasing number of smaller exhibitions of more peripheral design practitioners, or design phenomena, those which seem most useful ventures into unknown territory or which have a particularly interesting slant.

The Early Period, 1880 to 1914

Books, articles and papers

Adburgham, Alison. *Liberty's. A Biography of a Shop* (London, George Allen & Unwin, 1976)

Anscombe, Isabelle, and Gere, Charlotte. *Arts and Crafts in Britain and America* (London, Academy Editions, 1978)

Arts and Crafts Exhibition Society. *Arts and Crafts Essays* (London, Rivington Percival, 1893)

Ashbee, C.R. *Craftsmanship in Competitive Industry* (London, Grant & Co., for Essex House Press, 1908)

An Endeavour towards the Teaching of John Ruskin and William Morris (London, Essex House Press, 1901)

A Few Chapters in Workshop Reconstruction and Citizenship (London, Guild of Handicraft, 1894)

Memoirs (Unpublished typescript in Victoria and Albert Museum MSS Collection, 1938; original journals in King's College Library, Cambridge)

Should We Stop Teaching Art? (London, Batsford, 1912)

Aslin, Elizabeth. *The Aesthetic Movement: Prelude to Art Nouveau* (London, Elek, 1969)

19th Century English Furniture (London, Faber, 1962)

Benson, W.A.S. *Drawing: Its History and Uses*, with memoir by Hon. W.N.Bruce (Oxford University Press, 1925)

Benton, Charlotte, and Benton, Tim. *Form and Function. A Sourcebook for the History of Architecture and Design 1890–1939* (London, Crosby, Lockwood, Staples for Open University, 1975)

Billcliffe, Roger. *Charles Rennie Mackintosh, Furniture and Interiors* (Guildford, Lutterworth Press, 1979)

Blomfield, Sir Reginald. *Memoirs of an Architect* (London, Macmillan, 1932)

Blount, Godfrey. *Arbor Vitae: A Book on the Nature and Development of Imaginative Design for the use of Teachers, Handicraftsmen and Others* (London, Dent, 1899)

The Science of Symbols (London, Arthur C. Fifield, 1905)

Blunt, Wilfred. *Cockerell* (London, Hamish Hamilton, 1942)

'England's Michelangelo': A Biography of Frederic Watts (London, Hamish Hamilton, 1975)

Burne-Jones, Georgiana. *Memorials of Edward Burne-Jones* (London, Macmillan, 1904)

Callen, Anthea. *Angel in the Studio: Women in the Arts and Crafts Movement, 1870–1914* (London, Astragal Books, 1979)

Clark, Fiona. *William Morris: Wallpapers and Chintzes* (London, Academy Editions, 1973)

Cobden-Sanderson, T.J. *The Arts and Crafts Movement* (London, Hammersmith Publishing Society, 1905)

Cosmic Vision (London, Richard Cobden-Sanderson, 1922)

Journals (London, Richard Cobden-Sanderson, 1926)

Comino, Mary. *Gimson and the Barnsleys* (London, Evans Brothers, 1980)

Cooper, John Paul. 'The Work of John Sedding, architect'. Series of articles in *Architectural Review*, vols. 3 and 4, 1898

Crane, Walter. *An Artist's Reminiscences* (London, Methuen, 1907)

William Morris to Whistler (London, G.Bell & Sons, 1911)

Crawford, Alan, and Bury, Shirley, intrs. *C.R.Ashbee: Modern Silverwork* (New edition, London, Weinreb, 1974)

Cross, A.J. *Pilkington's Royal Lancastrian Pottery and Tiles* (London, Richard Dennis, 1980)

Crow, Gerald H. 'William Morris Designer'. Special issue of *The Studio*, Winter 1934

Davey, Peter. *Arts and Crafts Architecture* (London, Architectural Press, 1980)

Davidson, Eleanor. *The Simpsons of Kendal* (Lancaster University Visual Arts Centre, 1978)

Day, Lewis F. *Everyday Art: Short Essays on the Arts Not-Fine* (London, Batsford, 1882)

Dresser, Christopher. *Principles of Art* (London, 1881)
   Principles of Decorative Design (London, Cassell, Peter & Galpin 1873)
   Studies in Design for House Decorators, Designers and Manufacturers (London, Cassell, Peter & Galpin, 1876)

Faulkner, Thomas. 'W.R.Lethaby: tradition and innovation', from *Design 1900–1960*, papers given at Newcastle Polytechnic Conference (Newcastle Polytechnic, 1976)

Fitzgerald, Penelope. *Edward Burne-Jones: A Biography* (London, Michael Joseph, 1975)

Floud, Peter. 'The inconsistencies of William Morris'. Article in *The Listener*, October 14, 1954
   'William Morris as an artist: a new view'. Article in *The Listener*, October 7, 1954

Furst, H.E.A. *Decorative Art of Frank Brangwyn* (London, John Lane, 1924)

Girouard, Mark. *Sweetness and Light: The Queen Anne Movement 1860–1900* (Oxford University Press, 1977)

Harrison, Martin, and Walters, Bill. *Burne-Jones* (London, Barrie and Jenkins, 1973)

Haslam, Malcolm. *The Martin Brothers, Potters* (London, Richard Dennis, 1978)

Heal's Catalogues, 1853–1934. (Newton Abbot, David & Charles, 1972)

Henderson, Philip. *William Morris* (London, Thames and Hudson, 1967)

Howarth, Thomas. *Charles Rennie Mackintosh* (London, Routledge & Kegan Paul, 1952; new edition, 1976)

Hughes, Graham. *Modern Silver, 1880–1967* (London, Studio Vista, 1967)

Jewson, Norman. *By Chance I Did Rove* (Kineton, Warwick, Roundwood Press, 1973)

Kornwolf, James D. *M.H.Baillie Scott and the Arts and Crafts Movement* (Baltimore, Johns Hopkins Press, 1972)

Lambourne, Lionel. *Utopian Craftsmen* (London, Astragal Books, 1980)

Larner, Gerald and Celia. *The Glasgow Style* (Edinburgh, Paul Harris, 1979)

Lethaby, W.R. *Architecture. An introduction to the History and Theory of Building* (Williams & Norgate, 1912; new edition, Oxford University Press, 1955)
   Architecture, Mysticism and Myth (Percival & Co., 1892; new edition, London, Architectural Press, 1975)
   Form in Civilisation: Collected Papers in Art and Labour (Oxford University Press, 1922, reprinted 1957)
   Home and Country Arts (London, Home & Country, 1924)
   Philip Webb and his work (London, Oxford University Press, 1935; new edition, introduced by Godfrey Rubens, London, Raven Oak Press, 1979)

Lethaby, W.R. and others. *Ernest Gimson, his Life and Work* (Stratford-upon-Avon, Shakespeare Head Press, 1924)

Mackail, J.W. *The Life of William Morris* (London, Longmans Green, 1899)

Mackmurdo, A.H. History of the Arts and Crafts Movement (Unpublished manuscript in collection of William Morris Gallery, Walthamstow)

Macleod, Robert. *Charles Rennie Mackintosh* (London, Country Life, 1968)

Massé, H.J.L. *The Art Workers' Guild* (Oxford, Shakespeare Head Press, 1935)

Miller, Alec. C.R.Ashbee and the Guild of Handicraft (Unpublished typescript in Victoria and Albert Museum MSS Collection, c.1952)

Morris, May. *Introductions to the Collected Works of William Morris* (Separate edition, New York, Oriole Editions; London, Journeyman Press, 1973)

William Morris: Artist Writer Socialist (Oxford, Shakespeare Head Press, 1936; new edition, New York, Russell & Russell, 1966)

Morris, William. *Architecture, Industry and Wealth. Collected Papers* (London, Longmans Green, 1902)

Collected Works (London, Longmans Green, 1910–15)

Lectures (London, Longmans, 1898–1901)

Morton, Jocelyn. *Three Generations in a Family Textile Firm* (London, Routledge & Kegan Paul, 1971)

Muthesius, Hermann. *Das englische Haus* (Berlin, Wasmuth, 1904–5; English edition, *The English House*, St Albans, Granada/Crosby Lockwood Staples, 1979)

Naylor, Gillian. *The Arts and Crafts Movement* (London, Studio Vista, 1971)

Nuttgens, Patrick. 'A full life and an honest place', chapter on the Arts and Crafts in *Spirit of the Age: Eight Centuries of British Architecture* (London, BBC Publications, 1975)

Okey, Thomas. *A Basketful of Memories* (London, J.M.Dent, 1930)

Pevsner, Nikolaus. *Pioneers of the Modern Movement* (London, Faber, 1936); new edition, *Pioneers of Modern Design* (Harmondsworth, Penguin, 1960)

The Sources of Modern Architecture and Design (London, Thames and Hudson, 1968)

Studies in Art, Architecture and Design, vol. 2, including Morris, Mackmurdo, Mackintosh, Voysey, Walton (London, Thames and Hudson, 1968)

'William Morris, C.R.Ashbee and the Twentieth Century'. Article in *Manchester Review*, vol.7, Winter 1956

Richards, J.M., and Pevsner, Nikolaus, eds. *The Anti-Rationalists*, including Mackintosh, Mackmurdo, Liberty, and Reynolds-Stephens (London, Architectural Press, 1973)

Rothenstein, William. *Men and Memories* (London, Faber, 1931–9; new edition, London, Chatto & Windus, 1978)

Rushton, James H. *Ruskin Pottery* (West Bromwich, Metropolitan Borough of Sandwell, 1975)

Ruskin, John. *Seven Lamps of Architecture* (London, Smith Elder, 1849)

Stones of Venice (London, Smith Elder, 1851–3)

Two Paths: being lectures on Art and its Application to Decoration and Manufacture (London, Smith Elder, 1859)

Savage, Peter. *Lorimer and the Edinburgh Craft Designers* (Edinburgh, Paul Harris, 1980)

Sedding, John D. *Art and Handicraft* (London, Kegan Paul, Trench, Trübner, 1893)

Shaw, Bernard. 'William Morris as I knew him', reprint of 1936 essay (London, William Morris Society, 1966)

Simpson, Duncan. *C.F.A. Voysey: an Architect of Individuality* (London, Lund Humphries, 1979)

Spencer, Isobel. *Walter Crane* (London, Studio Vista, 1975)

Spencer, Robin. *The Aesthetic Movement: Theory and Practice* (London, Studio Vista, 1972)

Stirling, Mrs A.M.W. *William De Morgan and his Wife* (London, Thornton Butterworth, 1922)

Thompson, Paul. *The Work of William Morris* (London, Heinemann, 1967)

Vallance, Aymer. *William Morris, his Art, Writings and Public Life. A Record* (London, Bell, 1897; new edition, 1909)

Voysey, C.F.A. *Individuality* (London, Chapman and Hall, 1915)
    Reason as a Basis of Art (London, Elkin Mathews, 1906)

Watkinson, Raymond. *Pre-Raphaelite Art and Design* (London, Studio Vista, 1970)
    William Morris as Designer (London, Studio Vista, 1967)

There is also a great deal of relevant material for this period in the *Architectural Review* (from 1897) and *The Studio* (from 1893); and the current Newsletters, Journals and occasional publications of the Decorative Arts Society, the Charles Rennie Mackintosh Society, the William Morris Society and the Victorian Society.

Catalogues

The Aesthetic Movement 1869–1890. Exhibition at Camden Arts Centre, London. (London, Academy Editions, 1973)

The Aesthetic Movement and the Cult of Japan (London, Fine Art Society, 1972)

Architect-Designers: Pugin to Mackintosh (London, Fine Art Society, 1981)

The Arts and Crafts Movement (London, Fine Art Society, 1973)

C.R.Ashbee and the Guild of Handicraft (Cheltenham Art Gallery and Museum, 1981)

Good Citizens' Furniture: The Works of Ernest and Sidney Barnsley (Cheltenham Art Gallery and Museum, 1976)

Birmingham Gold and Silver: Assay Office Centenary Exhibition (Birmingham City Museum and Art Gallery, 1973)

The Art of Frank Brangwyn (Brighton Polytechnic, 1980)

Frank Brangwyn: Centenary Exhibition (Cardiff, National Museum of Wales, 1967)

British 20th Century Studio Ceramics (London, Christopher Wood Gallery, 1980)

An Exhibition of Cotswold Craftsmanship (Cheltenham, Montpellier Rotunda, 1951)

The Doulton Story. Catalogue of exhibition at Victoria and Albert Museum (Stoke-on-Trent, Royal Doulton Tableware, 1979)

Christopher Dresser: 1834–1904 (London, Camden Arts Centre, 1979)

The Earthly Paradise. Exhibition of work of the Birmingham Group (London, Fine Art Society, 1969)

Ernest Gimson (Leicester Museums and Art Gallery, 1969)

Ernest Gimson and the Cotswold Group of Craftsmen. Catalogue of collection (Leicestershire Museums, 1969)

Homespun To Highspeed: A Century of British Design, 1880–1980 (Sheffield City Art Galleries, 1979)

Liberty's 1875–1975 (London, Victoria and Albert Museum, 1975)

Charles Rennie Mackintosh. Catalogue of exhibition at the Royal Scottish Museum (Edinburgh, Scottish Arts Council, 1968)

The Eccentric A.H.Mackmurdo, 1851–1942 (Colchester, The Minories, 1979)

Morris and Company 1861–1940. Catalogue of exhibition at Victoria and Albert Museum (London, Arts Council, 1961)

Morris and Company (London, Fine Art Society, 1979)

Morris & Company in Cambridge (Cambridge University Press, 1980)

Textiles by William Morris and Morris & Co, 1861–1940 (Birmingham Museums and Art Gallery, 1981)

The Mortons: Three Generations of Textile Creation (London, Victoria and Albert Museum, 1973)

Omar Ramsden, 1873–1939 (Birmingham City Museum and Art Gallery, 1973)

The Silver Studio Collection: A London Design Studio 1880–1963. Middlesex Polytechnic Exhibition (London, Lund Humphries, 1980)

Victorian and Edwardian Decorative Arts (London, Victoria and Albert Museum, 1952)

Victorian and Edwardian Decorative Art. The Handley-Read Collection (London, Royal Academy, 1972)

C.F.A.Voysey: architect and designer. Catalogue of exhibition at Brighton Art Gallery and Museum (London, Lund Humphries, 1978)

A Choice of Design 1850–1980: Fabrics by Warner & Sons Ltd (Braintree, Warner & Sons, 1981)

Partnership in Style: Edgar Wood and J.Henry Sellers (Manchester City Art Gallery, 1975)

The Middle Period, 1915 to 1939

Books, articles and papers

Arts and Crafts Exhibition Society. *Handicrafts and Reconstruction* (London, John Hogg, 1919)

Barman, Christian. *The Man Who Built London Transport: A Biography of Frank Pick* (Newton Abbot, David & Charles, 1979)

Bayley, Stephen. *In Good Shape: Style in Industrial Products, 1900 to 1960* (London, Design Council, 1979)

Baynes, Ken and Kate. *Gordon Russell* (London, Design Council, 1981)

Benton, Charlotte, and Benton, Tim. *Form and Function. A Sourcebook for the History of Architecture and Design 1890–1939* (London, Crosby Lockwood Staples for Open University, 1975)

Bertram, Anthony. *Design in Daily Life* (London, Methuen, 1938)

Bertram, Anthony, and others. 'Design in everyday things'. Series of articles in *The Listener*, 1933

Bliss, Douglas Percy. *Edward Bawden* (Godalming, Pendomer Press, 1979)

Blake, John and Blake, Avril. *The Practical Idealists: A History of Design Research Unit* (London, Lund Humphries, 1969)

Cantacuzino, Sherban. *Wells Coates* (London, Gordon Fraser, 1978)

Cardew, Michael, and others. *Michael Cardew: Collected Essays* (London, Crafts Advisory Committee, 1976)

Carrington, Noel. *Design and a Changing Civilisation* (London, John Lane, Bodley Head, 1935)

Industrial Design in Britain (London, George Allen & Unwin, 1976)

The Shape of Things: An Introduction to Design in Everyday Life (London, Nicholson & Watson, 1939)

Clark, Garth. *Michael Cardew* (London, Faber, 1978)

Cole, Barbie Campbell, and Benton. Tim, eds. *Tubular Steel Furniture* (London, Art Book Company, 1979)

Design in Modern Life. Accompanying pamphlet for series of broadcast talks (London, BBC, 1933)

Digby, George Wingfield: *The Work of the Modern Pottery in England* (London, John Murray, 1952)

Dowling, H.G. *A Survey of British Industrial Arts* (Benfleet, F.Lewis, 1935)

Dunn, Geoffrey. 'One hundred years of furniture'. Illustrated survey in *Cabinet Maker* centenary issue, September 1980

Faulkner, Peter. *William Morris and Eric Gill* (London, William Morris Society, 1975)

Fournier, Robert, ed. *David Leach: A Monograph* (Tanyard, Lacock, Fournier Pottery, 1977)

Gill, Eric. *Autobiography* (London, Jonathan Cape, 1940)

Gloag, John. *Design in Modern Life* (London, George Allen & Unwin, 1934)

Industrial Art Explained (London, George Allen & Unwin, 1934)

Green, A. Romney. Autobiographical fragments (Unpublished manuscript in Victoria and Albert Museum MSS Collection, c.1946)

Hanson, Brian. 'Singing the Body Electric with Charles Holden'. Article in *Architectural Review*, December 1975

Haworth-Booth, Mark. *E.McKnight Kauffer: a designer and his public* (London, Gordon Fraser, 1979)

Heal's Catalogues, 1853–1934 (Newton Abbot, David & Charles, 1972)

Heskett, John. *Industrial Design* (London, Thames and Hudson, 1980)

Hogben, Carol. *The Art of Bernard Leach* (London, Faber, 1978)

Holland, James. *Minerva at Fifty: The Jubilee History of the Society of Industrial Artists and Designers 1930–1980* (Westerham, Hurstwood Publications, 1980)

Holme, Geoffrey. 'Frank Brangwyn designs for British industry'. Article in *The Studio*, vol.100, 1930

Industrial Design and the Future (London, Studio, 1934)

Hughes, Graham. *Modern Silver, 1880 to 1967* (London, Studio Vista, 1967)

Johnson, Stewart. *Eileen Gray: Designer, 1879–1976* (London, Debrett, for Victoria and Albert Museum and Museum of Modern Art, New York, 1979)

Leach, Bernard. *A Potter's Book* (London, Evelyn, Adams & Mackay, 1967)

Martin, J.L., and Speight, Sadie. *The Flat Book* (London, Heinemann, 1939)

Meynell, Francis. *My Lives* (London, Bodley Head, 1971)

Mairet, Ethel. Notes, diaries, letters (Unpublished material in collection of Bath Crafts Study Centre)

Morton, Jocelyn. *Three Generations in a Family Textile Firm* (London, Routledge & Kegan Paul, 1971)

Pevsner, Nikolaus. *An Enquiry into Industrial Art in England* (Cambridge University Press, 1937)

'Omega'. Article on the Omega Workshops in *Architectural Review*, vol.90, 1941

Studies in Art, Architecture and Design, vol.2, including Pick, Russell and the DIA (London, Thames and Hudson, 1968)

Plummer, Raymond. 'Fitness for Purpose: the Story of the DIA'. Reprinted in *Design and Industry* conference papers (London, Design Council, 1980)

Read, Herbert. *Art and Industry. The Principles of Industrial Design* (London, Faber, 1934)

Richards, J.M. 'Towards a rational aesthetic'. Article in *Architectural Review*, vol.78, 1935

Rogers, J.C. *Modern English Furniture* (London, Country Life, 1930)

Rose, Muriel. *Artist Pottery in England* (London, Faber, 1955; new edition, 1970)

Russell, Gordon. *Designer's Trade* (London, George Allen & Unwin, 1968)

Looking at Furniture (London, Lund Humphries, 1964)

Sharp, Dennis, ed. *The Rationalists. Theory and Design in the Modern Movement* (London, Architectural Press, 1978)

Simon, Herbert. *Song and Words: A History of the Curwen Press* (London, George Allen & Unwin, 1973)

Smith, Hamilton T. 'The DIA: the Early Years'. Article in *Design for Today*, May 1935; reprinted in *DIA Yearbook*, 1975, Diamond Jubilee Edition

Spalding, Francis. *Roger Fry* (London, Elek/Granada, 1980)

Speaight, Robert. *The Life of Eric Gill* (London, Methuen, 1966)

Ward, Neville, and Ward, Mary. *Home in the Twenties and Thirties* (London, Ian Allan, 1978)

Williams-Ellis, Clough. *Architect Errant* (London, Constable, 1971)

Woodham, Jonathan. 'British Art in Industry in 1935'. Reprinted in *Design and Industry* conference papers (London, Design Council, 1980)

There is a great deal of generally relevant material for this period in the *Architectural Review*; *Commercial Art and Industry*, later *Art and Industry* (from 1926); *Design and Industries Association Journal* and *News Sheet* (from 1918); *Design in Industry*, published by DIA (1932), replaced by *Design for Today* (1933), later superseded by *Trend in Design of Everyday Things* (1936); *The Society of Industrial Artists Newsletter and Journal* (from 1930); *The Studio*. Also in the current publications of The Thirties Society and The Decorative Arts Society.

Catalogues

Phyllis Barron and Dorothy Larcher: Hand-block Printed Textiles (Bath, Crafts Study Centre, 1978)

Frank Brangwyn. Exhibition of Furniture designed for E.Pollard, Oxford Street (London, The Avenue Press, 1930)

The Art of Frank Brangwyn (Brighton Polytechnic, 1980)

British Art in Industry (London, Royal Academy, 1935)

British 20th Century Studio Ceramics (London, Christopher Wood Gallery, 1980)

Classics of Modern Design (London, Camden Arts Centre, 1977)

Wells Coates, Architect and Designer (Oxford Polytechnic, 1979)

Susie Cooper: Elegance and Utility. Catalogue of exhibition at Sanderson's, London (Barlaston, Josiah Wedgwood, 1978)

Claud Lovat Fraser (London, Victoria and Albert Museum, 1969)

The Worshipful Company of Goldsmiths as Patrons of their Craft 1919–53. Catalogue of collection at Goldsmiths' Hall (London, Worshipful Company of Goldsmiths, 1965)

Hampstead in the Thirties: A Committed Decade (London, Camden Arts Centre, 1974)

Sir Ambrose Heal, Centenary Exhibition (London, Heal's, 1972)

Homespun to Highspeed: A Century of British Design, 1880–1980 (Sheffield City Art Galleries, 1979)

Alec B.Hunter. Textile Designer and Craftsman (Braintree, Warner & Sons, 1979)

The Art of Bernard Leach (London, Victoria and Albert Museum, 1977)

The Modernist Rug 1928–1938 (Brighton, Royal Pavilion, Art Gallery and Museums, 1975)

Alastair Morton and Edinburgh Weavers (Scottish National Gallery of Modern Art, 1978)

The Mortons: Three Generations of Textile Creation (London, Victoria and Albert Museum, 1973)

Keith Murray. Catalogue of travelling exhibition (London, Victoria and Albert Museum, 1976)

Omega Workshops: Furniture, Textiles and Pottery 1913–1918. Catalogue of exhibition at Victoria and Albert Museum (London, Arts Council, 1946)

Elizabeth Peacock: Weaving (Bath, Crafts Study Centre, 1978)

Pel and Tubular Steel Furniture of the Thirties (London, Architectural Association, 1977)

Katharine Pleydell-Bouverie (Bath, Crafts Study Centre, 1980)

The Poole Potteries (London, Victoria and Albert Museum, 1978)

Eric Ravilious 1903–1942 (Colchester, The Minories, 1972)

Shelley Pottery (London, Geffrye Museum, 1980)

Thirties: British Art and Design Before the War (London, Hayward Gallery, 1979)

The Thirties. Progressive Design in Ceramics, Glass, Textiles and Wallpapers. Catalogue of travelling exhibition (London, Victoria and Albert Museum, 1975)

A Choice of Design 1850–1980: Fabrics by Warner & Sons Ltd. (Braintree, Warner & Sons, 1981)

The Modern Period, 1940 to 1980

Books, articles and papers

Archer, L. Bruce. *Systematic Method for Designers* (London, Council of Industrial Design, 1965)

Ashford, F.C. *Designing for Industry: Some Aspects of the Product Designer's Work* (London, Pitman, 1955)

Banham, Mary, and Hillier, Bevis, eds. *A Tonic to the Nation: Festival of Britain*

1951. Book accompanying 1976 commemorative exhibition at Victoria and Albert Museum (London, Thames and Hudson, 1976)

Barry, Sir Gerald. 'The Festival of Britain, 1951.' Cantor lectures reprinted in *JRSA*, August 1952

Barty, Ewan. *Management and Engineering Design* (London, Design Council, 1972)

Bayley, Stephen. *In Good Shape: Style in Industrial Products, 1900 to 1960* (London, Design Council, 1979)

Baynes, Ken. *Industrial Design and the Community* (London, Lund Humphries, 1967)

About Design (London, Design Council, 1976)

Baynes, Ken, ed. *Attitudes in Design Education* (London, Lund Humphries, 1969)

Baynes, Ken and Baynes, Kate. *Gordon Russell* (London, Design Council, 1981)

Beresford-Evans, J. *Form in Engineering Design* (Oxford, Clarendon Press, 1954)

Birks, Tony. *The Art of the Modern Potter* (London, Country Life, 1967)

Black, Professor Misha. 'The education of industrial designers'. Cantor lectures reprinted in *JRSA*, vol.113, 1965

'Engineering and Industrial Design'. Paper reprinted in *Transactions of the Institute of Mechanical Engineers*, vol.186, 1972

'The training of industrial designers'. Paper reprinted in report of *Conference on the Teaching of Engineering* (London, Institute of Engineering Designers, 1964)

Bradshaw, A.E. *Handmade Woodwork of the Twentieth Century* (London, John Murray, 1962)

Carrington, Noel. *Design and Decoration in the Home* (London, Batsford, 1952)

Casson, Hugh. 'Dreams and awakenings'. Chapter on post-war architecture and design in *Spirit of the Age: Eight Centuries of British Architecture* (London, BBC Publications, 1975)

Casson, Michael. *Pottery in Britain Today* (London, Alec Tiranti, 1967)

Clark, Garth. *Michael Cardew* (London, Faber, 1978)

Crawford, Alan, intr. *Robert Welch, Design in a Cotswold Workshop* (London, Lund Humphries, 1973)

Darwin, Robin. 'The Dodo and the Phoenix: the Royal College of Art since the war'. Paper reprinted in *JRSA*, vol.102, 1954

'The training of the industrial designer'. Paper reprinted in *JRSA*, vol.97, 1949

Dunn, Geoffrey. 'One hundred years of furniture'. Illustrated survey in *Cabinet Maker* centenary issue, September 1980

Farr, Michael. *The Council of Industrial Design*. Monograph written on occasion of Gran Premio Internazionale Award, La Rinascente, Milan (London, Council of Industrial Design, 1959)

Design in British Industry – A Mid-Century Survey (Cambridge University Press, 1955)

Frayn, Michael. 'The Festival of Britain'. Chapter in *The Age of Austerity*, eds Michael Sisson and Philip French (London, Hodder & Stoughton, 1963)

Gloag, John. *The Missing Technician in Industrial Production* (London, George Allen & Unwin, 1944)

Goldsmiths, The Worshipful Company of. *Modern British Silver* (London, Worshipful Company of Goldsmiths, 1963)

Gorb, Peter, ed. *Living by Design: Pentagram Design Partnership* (London, Lund Humphries, 1978)

Goslett, Dorothy. *Professional Practice for Designers* (London, Batsford, 1961)

Height, Frank. ' . . and cheap tin trays'. RCA professorial inaugural lecture (London, Royal College of Art, 1977)

Hennessey, Elizabeth. 'Terence Conran, International Designer.' Chapter in *The Entrepreneurs* (Newbury, Scope Books, 1980)

Heskett, John. *Industrial Design* (London, Thames and Hudson, 1980)

Hillier, Bevis. *Austerity Binge: the Decorative Arts of the Forties and Fifties* (London, Studio Vista, 1975)

Holland, James. *Minerva at Fifty: The Jubilee History of the Society of Industrial Artists and Designers 1930 to 1980* (Westerham, Hurstwood Publications, 1980)

Hughes, Graham. *Modern Silver, 1880 to 1967* (London, Studio Vista, 1967)

Jones, J.Christopher. *Design Methods: Seeds of Human Futures* (London, Wiley-Interscience, 1970)

Lyall, Sutherland. *Hille: 75 Years of British Furniture*. Book accompanying retrospective exhibition at Victoria and Albert Museum (London, Elron Press, 1981)

Mayall, W.H. *Industrial Design for Engineers* (London, Iliffe, 1967)
    Machines and Perception in Industrial Design (London, Studio Vista, 1968)

Middleton, Michael. *Group Practice in Design* (London, Architectural Press, 1967)

Nuttgens, Patrick. 'Learning to some purpose'. Paper given for SIAD/Burton Design Award, reprinted by Society of Industrial Artists and Designers, 1977

Papanek, Victor. *Design for the Real World. Making to Measure* (London, Thames and Hudson, 1972)

Plummer, Raymond. 'Fitness for Purpose: The Story of DIA'. Reprinted in *Design and Industry* conference papers (London, Design Council, 1980)

Rose, Muriel. *Artist Pottery in England* (London, Faber, 1955; new edition, 1970)

Russell, Gordon. *Designer's Trade* (London, George Allen & Unwin, 1968)
    'Skill'. Paper reprinted in *JRSA*, November 1978
    'What is good design?' Article in *Design*, January 1949
    'Work of the Royal Designers for Industry', Paper reprinted in *JRSA*, vol.97, 1948

Russell, Gordon, intr. *Design in the Festival* (London, HMSO, 1951)

Society of Industrial Artists. *Designers in Britain*. Review of work of members (London, Wingate, 1947, 1949, 1951; London, Deutsch, 1953, 1957, 1964, 1971)

Young, Dennis and Barbara. *Furniture in Britain Today* (London, Alec Tiranti, 1964)

There is a great deal of generally relevant material for this period in *Crafts*, published by the Crafts Advisory Committee, later the Crafts Council (from 1973); *Design*, published by the Council of Industrial Design, later Design Council (from 1949); *Design and Industries Association Yearbook*; *House & Garden*; *Society of Industrial Artists Journal*, later *The Designer*.

Catalogues

Britain Can Make It: Design '46. Survey of exhibits in Council of Industrial Design exhibition at Victoria and Albert Museum (London, HMSO, 1946)

British 20th Century Studio Ceramics (London, Christopher Wood Gallery, 1980)

Classics of Modern Design (London, Camden Arts Centre, 1977)

Collingwood/Coper. Rugs and wallhangings by Peter Collingwood, Pots by Hans Coper (London, Victoria and Albert Museum, 1969)

Crafts Council Collection Catalogue of acquisitions (London, Crafts Council, 1980)

The Craftsman's Art. Crafts Advisory Council exhibition (London, Victoria and Albert Museum, 1973)

Design at Work: An Introduction to the Industrial Designer. Catalogue of Royal Designers for Industry exhibition at Royal Academy (London, Royal Society of Arts and Council of Industrial Design, 1948)

The Festival of Britain: Catalogue of exhibits, South Bank Exhibition (London, HMSO, 1951)

Homespun to Highspeed: A Century of British Design, 1880 to 1980 (Sheffield City Art Galleries, 1979)

Enid Marx: A Retrospective Exhibition (London, Camden Arts Centre, 1979)

Masterpiece: A Jubilee Exhibition of Crafts (London, Crafts Advisory Council, 1977)

Lucie Rie (London, Arts Council, 1967)

Utility Furniture and Fashion 1941–1951 (London, Geffrye Museum, 1974)

A Choice of Design 1850–1980: Fabrics by Warner & Sons Ltd (Braintree, Warner & Sons, 1981)

The Way We Live Now: Designs for Interiors 1950 to the Present Day (London, Victoria and Albert Museum, 1978)

British design collections

It is all very well to read the books and see the pictures and sort through the transparencies: but British design history has another vital element. It is, after all, a question of *objects*. There is no substitute for looking at the thing before you. Ten minutes spent examining a Gimson sideboard tells you more about the Arts and Crafts than reading the most conscientious of dissertations. Once you see, face to face, a 1930s Ekco radio set, designed in modern style by Wells Coates or Serge Chermayeff, you begin to realise why, in their time, these designs appeared quite so startling, so exciting. Look at a Race chair and you can understand the Festival of Britain. The sense of immediacy is sometimes quite uncanny. To get the sharpest impression of the work of some of this century's most innovative and influential of designers, the high British design movement this book has been describing, it is worth searching it out in the museums and the galleries, the archives and the salerooms, as well as some of the historic houses of this period, in which British design can be viewed in total context. It is, for instance, revealing and inspiriting to watch the meticulous attention to detail in Lutyens' grand design for Castle Drogo; or to have a vista of Elizabeth Peacock's Dartington Hall banners, one of the great craft commissions of this century, hanging in the big romantic space for which they were intended.

The practical problems entailed in any survey of British design have already been outlined in the introduction, for we still lack a coherent national modern design collection. This list has no claims to be exhaustive; but it may suggest a few good starting-points. I have asterisked some collections I especially recommend.

Where the majority of the collection is usually on show and normally accessible, this has been categorised '*Public collection*'.

Where part of the collection is on show and some in store, this has been labelled '*Public/Study collection*'. Viewing the study collection will entail advance arrangements.

Where the category is '*Study collection only*', this indicates that, while serious researchers are allowed in, by arrangement, the casual visitor will not be welcomed.

In any case, in these days of curtailed grants and cut-down staffing, it is always wise, before embarking on a special journey, to check what opening hours will be, and which exhibits visible.

Bath

Crafts Study Centre, Holburne Museum,
University of Bath, Great Pulteney Street,
Bath, Avon
Public/Study collection*

A relatively new collection, opened in 1977, and still very much evolving, which at present concentrates on the period from 1920 to 1940, giving a unique insight into the development of British crafts between the two World Wars. The idea developed from discussions among craftsmen and crafts enthusiasts from the older generation who felt there should be some focal point where the work of major artist-craftsmen of this century could be seen and studied in depth. The Centre is sponsored by the University of Bath and occupies part of the Holburne Museum, with exhibition and study areas purpose-designed by Neville Ward. The basis of the collection, which has been built up mainly through donations, many by the craftsmen themselves, consists of craft pottery, woven and printed textiles, calligraphy and furniture. Its highlights are the collection of almost 100 pots given by Bernard Leach himself and spanning his whole life's work; the marvellous hand-block prints of Phyllis Barron and Dorothy Larcher from the 1920s and 1930s; a substantial collection of Ethel Mairet's weaving, together with a great deal of useful source material, samples, notebooks, letters, photographs, from Ethel Mairet's workshop. It is the policy of the Centre, consistently and thoughtfully carried out, to focus attention on interesting areas hitherto neglected, such as the lady weavers of the 1920s; and a succession of changing exhibitions both reflects and stimulates research in progress.

Beaminster

Parnham House, Beaminster, Dorset
Historic house open to public

John Makepeace, the furniture designer, moved into Parnham House, a historic Dorset mansion of great interest and beauty, in 1977. Parnham houses (in some style) the John Makepeace School for Craftsmen in Wood, a charitable foundation which trains young craftsmen, and also contains John Makepeace's own workshops, making one-off furniture to special commission. These workshops are on public view, together with changing displays of Makepeace furniture, much of it en route to customers and exhibitions, and frequent displays of work by other craftsmen. A friendly, eventful, very optimistic enterprise.

Bedford

The Cecil Higgins Art Gallery,
Castle Close, Bedford
Public/Study collection

In recent reorganisations at Bedford, the late nineteenth-century collection has, they say, been arranged in room settings 'to evoke the atmosphere of a late Victorian family home'. Some family home: for the main source for this collection was the famous, rich, exotic, highly personal selection of Victorian and Edwardian *objets d'art* amassed with such devotion by Charles and Lavinia Handley-Read, fanatic collectors of that period, and dispersed in 1972, after their tragic deaths. The emphasis is on the strange and the flamboyant: good metalwork; magnificently eccentric pottery, Doulton, Martin Brothers, Minton, Elton, superlative De Morgan. The general idiosyncrasy extends to the supporting collections: even Gimson and Voysey appear at their least straightforward. There are newly-acquired pieces of John Paul Cooper metalwork, and continuing the tradition of flamboyance on into modern pottery, a 'Fish and Tulips' bowl by Alison Britton, purchased in 1980. For me, the *pièce de résistance* of the collection is the delicate and yet spectacular embroidered screen with entwined floral decoration designed by William Morris or perhaps his daughter May.

Bibury

Arlington Mill Museum,
Bibury, Gloucestershire
Public collection

In this country-life museum in a restored mill-building in Bibury, the village William Morris once designated the most beautiful in England, there is a large room full of Arts and Crafts furniture, including, rather touchingly, Ernest Gimson's work-table (just as unpretentious as one might imagine). The extremes of Cotswold furniture are illustrated nicely by the Peter Waals walnut cabinet, smug, grandiose and splendid, and the Sidney Barnsley dresser, ostentatious in its plainness. Which, one might well wonder, was the real Cotswold style?

Birmingham

City Museum and Art Gallery,
Chamberlain Square, Birmingham
Public/Study collection

The Birmingham City collections have two main specialist areas: textiles and metalwork. The full scope of the holdings of Morris & Co. textiles, including not only the large narrative tapestries designed by Burne-Jones but also the vast and glorious variety of printed and woven Morris fabrics, was revealed in the 1981 exhibition 'Textiles by William Morris and Morris & Co.', much the largest exhibition on this subject ever organised. There is normally a good semi-permanent display of metalwork at Birmingham for although the quantity, and quality, of pieces actually owned is disappointing, there has been some judicious borrowing, and it is possible to trace in an interesting way the influence of the Arts and Crafts silversmiths on Birmingham trade metalwork. The local connection is also very evident in the large collection of Ruskin Art Pottery, from the works founded in 1898 in Smethwick. The Martin Brothers and De Morgan are well represented, the latter with a collection of 150 pieces recently acquired. Although, as in most national civic collections, there are few acquisitions from the post-Edwardian period, and furniture has been almost totally ignored, connoisseurs of British crafts c.1980 will be delighted to discover a new gallery of craftwork purchased for Birmingham by West Midlands Arts under the title 'A Certain Style', showing the work of such modern artist-craftsmen as the furniture-maker Fred Baier, the silversmiths Michael Lloyd and Malcolm Appleby, the potters Elizabeth Fritsch and Glenys Barton, the weaver Roger Oates.

Braintree

Warner & Sons Ltd,
2 Anglia Way, Chapel Hill, Braintree,
Essex
Study collection only

Warner & Sons have been energetically cataloguing and rearranging their large archive, which covers Warners' production of woven and printed furnishing fabrics from the mid-nineteenth century to the present day. Warners' is an interesting example of a firm which has always had a dual design policy: a consistently safe traditional bourgeois output as the background to a succession of fabrics commissioned from the avant-garde designers of the period, such as Godwin and Mackmurdo in the late nineteenth century and Marion Dorn in the 1930s. Marianne

Straub has worked regularly for Warners' in the post-World War II period. Alec Hunter, son of Edmund Hunter of the St Edmundsbury Weaving Works, was Warners' design manager from 1932 until his death in 1958. He was the subject of an exemplary small-scale exhibition organised recently by Warners', one of a series of travelling exhibitions based on material from the archive.

Brighton

Art Gallery and Museums
and The Royal Pavilion,
Brighton
*Public collection**

Adjacent as it is to the Brighton Royal Pavilion, the ultimate expression of the whimsical tradition in British design history, one might have predicted the Art Gallery collection would determinedly avoid the dull and deadpan, and it is in fact an inspiringly eclectic gathering-in of the decorative arts, English and Continental, between 1890 and 1960, with the emphasis (so far) on the pre-World War II period. The collection is laid out very stylishly, along with contemporary paintings and sculpture. The qualities of British design – well represented by some fine pieces of Voysey and the dining-room suite designed by Charles Rennie Mackintosh for the Bassett-Lowke country cottage – are pointed up by their proximity to the work of Gallé, Majorelle and Bugatti. The recent, and generous, Robertson Gift of *art nouveau* includes some excellent Arts and Crafts metalwork. But, from the point of view of British designers, the strength of the collection is really in the furniture, and in particular, perhaps, in two exceptional 1920s pieces: the architect's table in oak by Frank Brangwyn which marvellously exemplifies the continuing Arts and Crafts tradition, and the walnut and macassar ebony buffet (see illustration no.110) designed in 1928 by Serge Chermayeff which shows British design taking quite a different turning. It is worth a trip to Brighton to see those alone.

Bristol

City Art Gallery,
Queen's Road, Bristol
Public/Study collection

Bristol, the birthplace of E.W.Godwin, is, suitably, the place to go for Anglo-Japanese. The Art Gallery collection includes a group of 13 pieces of furniture designed by Godwin for Ellen Terry, bequeathed by their daughter Edith Craig. There is also some interesting furniture by Marcel Breuer, designed for Crofton Gane's Bristol house in the mid-1930s when Breuer worked in England, and a few examples of Utility. Art and studio pottery is reasonably well represented, with some especially good Staite Murray pieces in the loan collection. The metalwork has recently been greatly boosted by loans from the very perspicacious private collection of *art nouveau* and Arts and Crafts metalwork formed by a local expert, Dr K.C.P.Smith.

Broadway

Gordon Russell Ltd,
Broadway, Worcestershire
*Study collection only**

The Gordon Russell collection, a small museum section within the Broadway factory, is, in a way, my favourite of all design collections. It says so much about not just the evolution of Gordon Russell furniture but also the whole Gordon Russell design ethos, the tradition of the Cotswolds, the British design story. It has never been a formal, academic kind of collection but a collection which has accumulated very much at random, and this gives it a wonderful sense of authenticity. There are very good examples of all Gordon Russell periods, from the Arts and Crafts phase of the early 1920s to the 1930s' almost-international modernism, including the notorious Gordon Russell boot cupboard which, according to Pevsner, marked the turning-point in style. Later designs are to be seen not in the museum but in the factory showroom; some of the designs we now regard as post-World War II classics are in fact very much still in production. Besides the furniture, there is of course a collection of R.D.Russell's famous Murphy radio cabinets.

Cambridge

**Fitzwilliam Museum,
Trumpington Street,
Cambridge**
Public/Study collection*

The Fitzwilliam Museum, for me, comes near perfection: in size, in atmosphere, in its discriminating collecting, it is surely everything a museum ought to be. The Fitzwilliam has particular links with Morris and associates through Sydney Cockerell, its Director from 1908 to 1937. Cockerell had previously been Secretary to the Kelmscott Press and a kind of right-hand man William Morris, and the Morris collection at the Museum is, not surprisingly, remarkable: especially the printing, but also the furniture and textiles which were memorably brought together in the Fitzwilliam exhibition 'Morris & Company in Cambridge' in 1980. Though the collection on the whole is at its strongest in the Arts and Crafts period, including a few pieces of quite interesting metalwork, the small, but discerning, selection of studio pottery – Martin Brothers, Leach, Staite Murray, Coper, Rie, Mary White, Colin Pearson – continues to the present day.

**Kettle's Yard,
Northampton Street,
Cambridge**
Public collection*

Kettle's Yard began as a private collection made by Jim Ede, art connoisseur, author of the important book on Gaudier-Brzeska, and his wife Helen. These were the things they lived with. The collection is now administered by the University of Cambridge, but Kettle's Yard retains an intense, indeed an almost ghostly, atmosphere of domesticity in which the paintings, sculptures and works of craft mingle in immaculately casual near-to-real-life room sets. Some excellent pottery: Leach, Staite Murray, Katharine Pleydell-Bouverie, Robin Welch; engraved glass by David Peace; a rug by Roger Oates. A strange and slightly magic place.

Chagford

Castle Drogo, nr Chagford, Devon
National Trust House

Castle Drogo, the last of the Great Houses, was built by Sir Edwin Lutyens for Julius Drewe, Home and Colonial Stores tycoon, between 1910 and 1930. This colossal building, breathtakingly sited high above a gorge on a massive granite outcrop, is amazing not only for the total grandiosity of Lutyens' concept but also for his near-obsessive zest for detail which makes much twentieth-century design look namby-pamby. Even his design for a dish-rack in the kitchen is, in itself, a *tour de force*.

Cheltenham

Art Gallery and Museum,
40 Clarence Street, Cheltenham,
Gloucestershire
*Public collection**

The Cotswolds were the main rural outpost of Arts and Crafts activity at the turn of the century, and this is well reflected in the Cheltenham collection, built up gradually since the 1930s, which now has some magnificent examples of the period. The substantial collection of furniture by Sidney Barnsley and Ernest Gimson covers the whole spectrum from the very basic ash ladderback chairs, much used in simple life, to the grander, more ornate and intricately inlaid display pieces. There is some marvellous metalwork by Gimson, and the collection is backed up by a great many working drawings. A very impressive recent acquisition is the large Ward Higgs collection of furniture by Voysey, including the Swan chair and the Kelmscott Chaucer cabinet: especially interesting in the Cotswold context for it shows what was, in some ways, quite an opposite approach.

The Museum has pursued an enterprising policy in the past few years of important exhibitions of Cotswold-orientated Arts and Crafts: 'Good Citizens' Furniture, The Work of Ernest and Sidney Barnsley' in 1976; 'C.R.Ashbee and the Guild of Handicraft' in 1981.

Dudley

Broadfield House Glass Museum,
Kingswinford, Dudley, West Midlands
Public collection

The top two rooms of this new museum, a suburban department of Dudley Art Gallery, concentrate on the glass of the past century: mainly late nineteenth-century industrial production of the Stourbridge area, but also, increasingly, modern studio glass from the growing number of British craft glass workshops.

East Grinstead

Standen, East Grinstead, Sussex
National Trust House

Standen was built by Philip Webb, the father figure of Arts and Crafts architects, in 1894. It is a picturesque and pleasant building, perhaps a bit more quirky than one might have expected from the man who liked his work to appear absolutely ordinary, but predictably full of the special atmosphere, the peculiar combination of the rich and decorative with the pure and the highminded, which was such a feature of that period in design. It does much for one's understanding of the movement to see the Morris & Co. furniture and carpets in situ, rather worn, and the Morris wallpaper, some of it original, some more recently reprinted by Sanderson's using the old blocks. Around the house, there is much decorative pottery, especially De Morgan; lamps by Benson; furniture designed by Ashbee for the Guild of Handicraft: a coherent, vivid collection gradually being added to by the very knowledgeable National Trust tenant at Standen, Arthur Grogan.

Exeter

Royal Albert Memorial Museum,
Queen Street, Exeter
Public collection

The craft collection – pottery and glass – was begun at Exeter in the early 1940s with a large gift from the Contemporary Art Society. It covers the great modern potters, Leach, Staite Murray, Cardew, Pleydell-Bouverie; and it also has a local bias, with contemporary work from such south-western potters as Marianne de Trey, Peter Starkey and Svend Bayer.

Gateshead

Shipley Art Gallery,
Prince Consort Road, Gateshead,
Tyne and Wear
Public collection

The collection at Gateshead is a very good example of a growing national trend: the gradual building up of modern crafts collections with the help of Regional Arts associations. The Permanent Collection of Contemporary British Craft (as they call it in Shipley), established in 1976, financed partly by the local authority and partly by Northern Arts, is a deliberately general one, including pottery by Lucie Rie, Gordon Baldwin, Alison Britton, Mary Rogers; glass by George Elliott, Pauline Solven, Dillon Clarke; tapestry by Archie Brennan; and a good selection of modern jewellery. Much of the work is being bought direct from craftsmen, and some has been specially commissioned for the collection.

Glasgow

Art Gallery and Museum,
Kelvingrove, Glasgow
Public/Study collection

All C.R.Mackintosh's major buildings are in Glasgow, and so are the main public collections of his work. The Kelvingrove Museum houses the furnishings from the Ingram Street Tea-Rooms, from the tables and chairs, in considerable variety, down to the specially-made silverplated cutlery. The Museum has embarked on an interesting policy of collecting furniture in the form of room-sets, with the intention of eventually displaying the history of modern interior design from the Mackintosh period to the present day. So far, among their acquisitions is furniture designed in the early 1900s for a house in Birmingham by Edward Taylor, a Glasgow designer contemporary with Mackintosh, the husband of the illustrator Jessie King; and also the bedroom and lounge furniture from a house in Southgate designed in the late 1920s. The bedroom is by E.Arthur Brown; the lounge by Gordon Russell, including an excellent Marian Pepler carpet.

Hill House, Helensburgh, Glasgow
*House owned by the Royal
Incorporation of Architects in Scotland,
open to the public**

Hill House, a lovely building in best Mackintosh-suburban, commissioned by the publisher Walter Blackie in 1902, is one of the best places to see Mackintosh's furniture, as an essential part of his interior. Hill House is, in a sense, a building of extremes: the white bedroom, the black drawing room; the quickly-changing spaces of the corridors and stairways; the elongated forms; startling motifs of decoration. It is full of surprises, down to the smallest detail. But the final impression is anything but restless. The house has great coherence, an extraordinary stillness of atmosphere, romantic and evocative. It is nicely cared for, and a joy to wander through.

Glasgow School of Art,
Renfrew Street, Glasgow
*Study collection only**

Much the most spectacular example of Charles Rennie Mackintosh in action is this amazing building. It was designed by Mackintosh, in two phases, between 1897 and 1909, and it is still very much a working art school. It shows all Mackintosh's guiding principles of structure and decoration at their most impressive and also their most subtle: it is a building of immense sophistication. Besides the well-known landmarks – the Director's Room, the 'Hen Run', the much-photographed, much-televised tall, galleried School Library – and the many built-in details, ironwork and clocks and furniture, which give the School of Art its extraordinary character, a separate collection of furniture by Mackintosh has gradually accumulated, through a sequence of gifts from Mackintosh aficionados, and a few perceptive purchases by the School itself. The furniture is kept, in pleasantly informal setting, in the Mackintosh Room within the Art School, and it is an especially rewarding collection, with some marvellous pieces of early Mackintosh in the 'Spooky School' style so much derided by contemporary mainstream English Arts and Crafts designers.

Hunterian Art Gallery,
The University, Glasgow
*Public collection**

The largest and most highly representative collection of Charles Rennie Mackintosh's work is owned by the University of Glasgow. The basis of the collection was acquired in the mid-1940s and, with the addition of later gifts and purchases, it now amounts to over 600 drawings, watercolours and designs as well as more than 60 pieces of furniture. But it is only recently, with the opening of the University's new Hunterian Art Gallery, that this major collection has been put on show. The purpose-designed Mackintosh wing at the Hunterian, opened in 1981, is in effect a curious kind of reparation for the destruction by the University of 78 Southpark Avenue in Glasgow, which had been the Mackintoshes' house from 1906 to 1913: the University had kept and stored much of the interior, and the original panelling and fitted furniture has been used to make a facsimile reconstruction of 78 Southpark Avenue at the Hunterian. Reinstated in the room in which he used to sit at it is Charles Rennie Mackintosh's own writing cabinet, sold at Sotheby's for the record sum of £89,200, in 1979, and later bought back by Glasgow University after a public appeal. Besides the important Southpark Avenue material, there is the well-known white bedroom furniture from Mains Street, and Mackintosh furniture exhibited, and much acclaimed, in turn-of-the-century Vienna and Turin. The complete suite of rather later bedroom furniture, designed in 1919 for the Bassett-Lowke house, 78 Derngate, Northampton, shows Mackintosh's style in what might have been a striking stage of evolution, half way to modernism. But alas this was to be his last sizeable commission.

Guildford

The Watts Gallery,
Compton, near Guildford, Surrey
Public collection

G.F.Watts, alias 'England's Michelangelo', was one of the most highly-revered Victorian painters, and his wife Mary, also an artist, was very much embroiled in the Home Arts and Industries activities of the late nineteenth century. Shortly before Watts' death in 1904, she started her own local rural industry, the Potters' Art Guild, and the wares of the Guild were sold commercially, notably through Liberty's. Their Celtic-motif garden pots won prizes in their day. In and around the Watts Gallery at Compton there are examples of Potters' Art Guild work, but the best display of all is at the nearby Compton Mortuary Chapel, designed by Mary Watts, with terracotta decorations carried out by the villagers under her direction. The interior of the Chapel is ornate and very complex, Art and Crafts at its most vivid and symbolic. Mary Watts herself described it as 'glorified wallpaper'. She greatly underestimated its effect.

Hove

**Museum of Art,
19 New Church Road, Hove,
Sussex**
Public collection

Augmenting their major collections of eighteenth- and nineteenth-century ceramics, Hove Museum has a small but steadily growing group of modern studio pottery – by Lucie Rie, Quentin Bell, Joanna Constantinides, Derek Davies, Jacqueline Poncelet and other practitioners, some local – and a few good pieces of contemporary glass.

Kendal

**Abbot Hall Art Gallery,
Kendal, Cumbria**
Study collection only

In twentieth-century handmade woodwork, there have been two main lines of descent: the Gimson/Barnsley line which descends to Edward Barnsley and the craftsmen who trained with him, including Alan Peters; and the Romney Green tradition which goes down to Stanley Davies (of the two, the Romney Green is the most strongly intellectual). The Abbot Hall Art Gallery has been most fortunate in recently acquiring a collection of choice pieces of Stanley Davies furniture. Davies worked for many years in Windermere, and made the bequest, which includes many working drawings and photographs, shortly before he died in 1977. The Museum also owns a few examples of furniture by Simpson's of Kendal, local craft workshops who made furniture for C.F.A. Voysey (among others); and it is hoped that these two complementary collections will eventually be seen on permanent display together.

Lechlade

**Kelmscott Manor,
Kelmscott, nr Lechlade, Oxfordshire**
*House owned by the Society of
Antiquaries of London, regularly, but
infrequently, open to the public**

Kelmscott Manor was Morris's ideal style of building: unpretentious yet dignified Cotswold vernacular with stone roofs and wide gables and great yew trees in the garden. Although in the beginning his tenancy there was ill-fated and unhappy, for he shared the building with Rossetti, a most uneasy ménage, he grew to love it more and more as he got older, and his daughter May lived on there until she died in 1938. Kelmscott, in recent years, has been extremely well restored by the Society of Antiquaries. It is full of atmosphere. It is also full of treasures: paintings by Rossetti; furniture by Philip Webb and the box-like green-painted bedroom furniture designed by Ford Madox Brown at his most workmanlike. The chief glory of the collection at Kelmscott is the superb embroidery, the best assembly anywhere of hangings, covers, curtains, designed and (mostly) carried out within the Morris family: from the famous 'Daisy' hanging worked by William and Jane Morris not long after their marriage to the magnificent bed curtains designed by May Morris for her father a few years before he died.

Leeds

**Lotherton Hall,
Aberford, near Leeds, West Yorkshire**
*Public collection**

The most interesting modern craft collection in the north, indeed I think the best in any civic gallery, is centred at Lotherton Hall, a not, in itself, especially distinguished Edwardian country mansion given to Leeds by Sir Alvery and Lady Gascoigne in 1968. With the house came a generous endowment, which has allowed Leeds City

Art Gallery, which administers the house, to build up a considerable collection not only of pieces from the late Victorian and Edwardian periods – a fine Gimson corner cupboard was an early acquisition – but also contemporary crafts and modern fashion, assembled with great expertise and sense of style. The ceramics are especially impressive: some very good examples of Fritsch, Britton, Rie, Coper, Glenys Barton; and a charming series of 'Lotherton Hall' tiles in porcelain, incised and painted by Kate Wickham. The modern collection has a few exceptional textiles – a particularly beautiful Eng Tow quilted hanging – and a sensitive selection of modern furniture from Fred Baier, Eric de Graaf and David Colwell. The excellent Museum Shop furniture, and furnishings and showcases for the new Oriental Gallery, were specially commissioned from Jack Hardy, whose workshops are in Penistone, nearby.

Leicester

Leicestershire Museum and Art Gallery,
New Walk, Leicester
Public/Study collection*

Ernest Gimson, the most influential furniture designer of this century, was born in Leicester, and the very large collection of his work at the Leicestershire Museum began in the year of his death, 1919, when Gimson's widow presented his drawings for the new federal capital of Australia (not built: or, anyway, not built as Gimson planned it). The nucleus of Gimson relatives and patrons around Leicester have been generous in giving examples of his work and the work of Gimson's colleagues, with the result that Leicester now has one of the two major national collections of the furniture of Gimson, Sidney and Ernest Barnsley and Peter Waals. (The other major collection is at Cheltenham, *q.v.*) Leicester owns a number of prize pieces, several of which are illustrated in this book: for instance Gimson's superb macassar ebony cabinet inlaid with mother-of-pearl (on page 69); the massive three-sided plain oak cupboard with brass handles which belonged to Harry Peach (page 73); Ernest Barnsley's mediaevalist oak chest with light oak floral inlay (page 64). Besides, you will find many smaller, less obtrusive pieces, still impeccable in detail, which tell you a great deal about the Gimson way of doing things. There is some of Gimson's plasterwork, embroidery and metalwork; and the whole collection is described and illustrated in Annette Carruthers' very good and careful catalogue.

Liverpool

Merseyside County Museums,
William Brown Street,
Liverpool
Public/Study collection

Merseyside is becoming a serious centre for the study of twentieth-century studio ceramics. The Museum for some years has had a reasonable coverage of the early period (Ruskin, Doulton, Della Robbia) and the 1920s and 1930s (Charles Vyse, Reginald Wells, Bernard Leach, Katharine Pleydell-Bouverie). More recently, with the help of the Crafts Council, the Museum has begun buying steadily from modern potters (Batterham, Fritsch, Caiger-Smith, Ewen Henderson, Michael Cardew, Mary Rogers), and expanding their ceramics-orientated study services. A changing selection of twentieth-century studio and workshop pottery is always on display.

Williamson Art Gallery and Museum,
Slatey Road, Birkenhead
Public collection

The Della Robbia pottery company, founded in Birkenhead in 1894 by Harold Rathbone, was one of those poignantly short-lived enterprises of the Arts and Crafts period, age of high ideals. It was probably hoping for too much to start reworking the aesthetic principles of Italian Renaissance pottery in turn-of-the-century Birkenhead. The pottery closed down again in 1906, in financial trouble. But not without producing some memorable pottery, Italianate but also very English, strong, flamboyant, a good collection of which is at the Williamson, a suitable tribute to a unique local venture.

London

Crafts Council,
12 Waterloo Place, London SW1
Study collection, a large proportion of which is frequently on exhibition around the country*

One of the original ideas when the Crafts Advisory Committee (which became the Crafts Council) was founded in 1971 was to earmark a proportion of its funds for actually purchasing work from modern craftsmen. The resulting collection, which is rapidly expanding, with a total at present of around 600 objects, is intended to be a working collection, for use for loans to museums and arts centres and for special exhibitions. It is (unlike the collection at the Bath Crafts Study Centre, which tends to concentrate on the between-wars period) emphatically a contemporary collection: its earliest objects are two bowls by Lucie Rie which date from the mid-1950s, and most of the collection in fact consists of pieces from the 1970s and 1980s, selected – and, needless to say, severely argued over – by a changing committee of these same modern craftsmen. The committee's main guide-line is that of quality, to buy the best they can, and on the whole this works effectively. Almost all the major names in contempory crafts are represented by some quite distinguished pieces: which is surely as much as one can hope for (maybe more). The collection's shortcomings in fact are mainly technical. Furniture, one feels, is rather under-represented, presumably because of storage and transport problems. Metalwork, as in so many modern collections, is meagre; though the Crafts Council jewellery collection is a strong one. It is perhaps, however, an accurate reflection of the state of British crafts that the silversmiths and glassmakers are poorly represented compared with the producers of textiles and ceramics. Good weavers and good potters are much thicker on the ground.

Geffrye Museum,
Kingsland Road, London E2
Public/Study collection

This original and intriguing museum, housed in the now vacated eighteenth-century almshouses of the Ironmongers' Company, has a permanent display of period rooms showing the development of the middle-class British home from about 1600 onwards. The sequence of the styles includes a room of furniture by Voysey, genteel Arts and Crafts in ambience. (Whistler once denounced an interior by Ashbee as an example of the disastrous effect of art upon the middle classes: he might well have done the same for Voysey.) Another bourgeois room has furniture by Gordon Russell, in the played-down modern style of Broadway, Worcs., in the 1930s. It is to be hoped that the powers at the Geffrye soon decide to disinter Utility, of which they have an excellent collection in the basement, to make a room which shows the English style in wartime. It was at the Geffrye that the first retrospective exhibition of Utility was held in 1974.

Goldsmiths' Hall,
Foster Lane, London EC2
Study collection, some of it on show to
the public during exhibitions*

The Worshipful Company of Goldsmiths has much the largest and by far the most remarkable collection of modern British silver in the country, built up assiduously from the 1920s onwards first by George Hughes, Art Secretary and later Clerk to the Company, and then by his son Graham, who was Art Director from 1953 to 1981. Though the Goldsmiths' Hall collection is relatively thin on the late Victorian and Edwardian periods, apart from some good Dresser and a lovely double-handled silver sugar bowl by Ashbee, it comes into its own in the mid-1920s, with superb pieces by Gleadowe, H.G.Murphy, Harold Stabler and, a classic of its period, the Goldsmiths' Hall cigar box in grey shagreen designed by John Paul Cooper (this is illustrated on page 93). The post-war collection is equally impressive. The Goldsmiths' Company carried on its policy of commissioning pieces from the leading modern craftsmen, and 1960s silversmiths – Gerald Benney, David Mellor, Robert Welch – are well represented not only by their specially commissioned one-off pieces, some of them spectacular, but also by their metalwork designs for mass production. This means that, as well as being a main source for modern silverwork, the Goldsmiths' Company has an interesting collection of early British modern stainless steel.

Heal & Son Ltd,
196 Tottenham Court Road,
London W1
Study collection only

In a rooftop storeroom, high above its sales floors of modern furniture, Heal's keep a small collection of historic furniture, which is occasionally brought out on exhibition. It contains good examples of all the main Heal periods: Heal Arts and Crafts style of the 1890s/1900s (see the plain and simple washstand on page 67, part of the Heal collection); Heal DIA-functional of the post-World War I era; the fumed oak furniture of the later 1920s, when Heal designs were turning a bit more neo-Georgian; the Heal modernist phase; a few 'contemporary' pieces. An important little collection, unique and very personal.

Kingston upon Thames Museum
and Art Gallery,
Fairfield West, Kingston upon Thames
Public/Study collection

Kingston acquired the prestigious Ernest Marsh ceramics collection in 1945. Ernest Marsh was a great expert in this area, and he had collected some wonderful examples of English studio pottery, from Fishley of Fremington and Cox of Mortlake to Wells of Chelsea, Bernard Leach, William Staite Murray. The greatest part of the collection is the Martinware: almost 80 pieces, not so much grotesques as jugs and vases, jars and teapots, chosen with a connoisseur's discrimination. It seems, to say the least, a pity that 35 years after the acquisition of a collection of this stature only a small proportion is on public exhibition.

Leighton House Art Gallery and
Museum,
12 Holland Park Road, Kensington,
London W14
Public collection

The house where Lord Leighton used to live is one of the most fantastical, romantic buildings in London. The authentically reconstructed Arab Hall, designed as an integral part of the building by the architect George Aitchison, is an amazing spectacle, in which the genuinely oriental tiles shipped in by Lord Leighton and his friends from Rhodes, Damascus, Cairo and so on, are mingled with the quasi-Oriental work of the Arts and Crafts designers Walter Crane and William De Morgan. Besides his tiles (in situ), there is a very large (and more free-standing) collection of De Morgan's highly decorative pottery, presented to Leighton House by Mrs Perrin, a long-term De Morgan admirer and supporter, and now owned by the Borough of Kensington and Chelsea. This is always on show at Leighton

House, together with the work of Leighton himself and other artists of the period, and good late Victorian furniture: a High Victorian shrine of great resplendence. As well as the Leighton House holding of De Morgan, there is a substantial collection in the keeping of the London Borough of Hammersmith and Fulham, at Fulham District Library; but this is a study collection, and access is very limited. The large and particularly splendid De Morgan Trust collection, covering the whole Chelsea – Merton Abbey-Fulham cycle, which used to be on show at Old Battersea House but which was dispersed when the London Borough of Wandsworth sold the building, is at present, sad to say, in packing cases, and plans for its future are apparently still vague.

Middlesex Polytechnic, Bounds Green Road, London N11
Study collection only

Almost by chance, in 1967, as a result of an article in *The Guardian*, Middlesex Polytechnic acquired a gargantuan collection of the work and records of the Silver Studio, one of the earliest and most prolific commercial design studios. Between 1880 and 1963, the Studio produced nearly 30,000 designs, mostly for furnishing textiles and wallpapers, but also for plasterwork, dress fabrics, metalwork, furniture, even complete interiors, some under its own name, some incognito. They could turn their hand to anything. As John Brandon-Jones commented in the foreword to the excellent (and, mercifully, quite selective) centenary exhibition organised in 1980 by the Polytechnic: 'In the Silver Studio Exhibition we can, at last, see the work of one of the greatest Ghost organisations ever to work in the field of applied art'.

Victoria and Albert Museum, Cromwell Road, South Kensington, London SW7
Public/Study collection*

For those with the stamina to seek them out through the maze of Primary Galleries, Study Collections and subterranean storerooms, the Victoria and Albert Museum has some prime examples of the work of almost all the major designers in this area in the last hundred years. The British modern collections at the v & a have, so far, had a somewhat chequered history. Though the early modern designers, the designers of the Aesthetic Movement and first phase of Arts and Crafts, have been relatively secure, in the safe keeping of a departmental network responsible for all collections up to 1900, the twentieth century has been rather an anomaly, the fief of the Circulation Department, which organised the Museum's travelling exhibitions; the modern collections only recently reverted to the individual departments, when the Circulation Department was closed down.

Because of its past history, especially the fact that collecting has tended to be focused on the special needs and pressures of current exhibitions, the collection has particular strengths in some directions – its coverage, for instance, of the work of Keith Murray, subject of an exhibition in the 1970s, is peculiarly intensive – but in other areas it can be relatively patchy. There are many signs, however, of new energy and interest in overhauling totally the modern collections at South Kensington, both the representation of industrial design and crafts from individual workshops. One useful move has been the assembly of a 20th Century Study Collection which, although displayed in a rather disconcertingly uncompromising manner, Anti-Display at its most blatant, at least helps identify the collection's strengths and weaknesses: at long last one can see what it, more or less, consists of. Plans for the imminent opening of a large new 20th Century Primary Gallery, an international design collection, 1903 to 1950, in a prestige position near the Museum entrance, together with the stimulus of activities at the Conran Foundation Boilerhouse (*q.v.*) should, within the next few years, make the V & A the obvious major centre for contemporary design: which was, after all, how Sir Henry Cole intended it. Indeed it could have important influence on how design develops in Britain from now on.

In detail, in spite of sundry oddnesses and weakness, the collections are of an extraordinary quality.

The Furniture and Woodwork Department, in the 19th Century Primary Galleries, has some wonderful pieces of Arts and Crafts, with more in the 20th Century Study Collection where the bulk of modern furniture is shown. From the early period, there are excellent examples of Godwin, Mackmurdo, Voysey, George Walton, C.R.Ashbee and a stunning Ballie Scott piano which the Museum has quite recently acquired. The Cotswold School is rather weakly represented, but there is good Heal and a positive profusion of Omega Workshops furniture. A strong collection from the late 1920s/1930s: good Isokon; an interesting dining set for mass production by the Bath Cabinet Co.; the best piece of 1930s Gordon Russell to be seen in any public collection; quite a lot from the Festival of Britain period and onwards, though so far the assortment seems to be a little random. The new craft revival furniture is represented with, for instance, a fine eccentric cabinet by Makepeace and a bench especially commissioned (to be sat on) by the V & A from Richard La Trobe-Bateman.

The Metalwork Department works to rather the same pattern, with its prize exhibits of the Victorian period on show in the 19th Century Primary Galleries; with somewhat lesser pieces and with modern metalwork in the specialised Metalwork Galleries; and, of course, with a great deal more in store. One can normally expect to find a very complete collection of late nineteenth/early twentieth-century metalwork: Dresser, Liberty, Ramsden, Benson, John Paul Cooper, C.R.Mackintosh, George Walton Cutlery (page 81). Ashbee's Guild of Handicraft is a Museum speciality, and the Birmingham Guild is well represented too. The collection has fine pieces from the Arts and Crafts enamellers; e.g. an especially superb Nelson Dawson enamelled cup and cover. In the 1920s/1930s period, although the Museum has good pieces here and there, including a fascinating Harold Stabler tea-set, the coverage on the whole is less convincing; here, the Goldsmiths' Hall collection leaves it standing. But it gathers strength once again in the post-war period, with examples of the silver of the 1950s/1960s (Robert Goodden's Festival of Britain tea-set, David Mellor's Embassy, for instance) alongside mass-produced metalwork of that same era; and some magnificent very recent pieces, an enamelled silver jug by Gerald Benney, silver candelabra by Robert Welch, specially commissioned for the Museum collection.

The Ceramics Department is, like the other collections at the V & A, extremely well endowed with designs from the late Victorian period, some of which are on show in the 19th Century Primary Galleries and some of which are displayed in the departmental collections. The Ceramics Galleries, even more than most, suffer from an *embarras de richesses*, and the juxtapositions in the overcrowded showcases can, almost by accident, prove tremendously illuminating: you find handwork cheek by jowl with industrial production, and the examples from the 1920s/1930s are, in this respect, particularly interesting. The V & A has a massive, though uneven, collection of British studio pottery, from the Martin Brothers onwards, and it is still buying. Work by very modern potters – Elizabeth Fritsch, Alison Britton and Jill Crowley, for example – have recently been added. Though the 20th century industrial glass collection is sketchy, really hardly worth the detour, there has been a steady policy of purchases in the more idiosyncratic studio glass areas, mainly from the Glasshouse group – Taylor, Solven, Tookey, Meech, Clarke, Newell – over the last few years.

The modern collection of the Textile Department at the V & A is, predictably enough, one of the strongest in the country. (The only textiles collection comparable in range and quality is at the Whitworth in Manchester, *q.v.*) At any one time, around 200 designs are on view in the Textile Study Room of the Museum, with an immense backing stock to draw on. The Aesthetic Movement, the Arts and Crafts, the modernists are all superbly well represented; the extent and the high quality of 1930s coverage was indicated in 'The Thirties' exhibition at the Hayward in 1979. (The span of the collections up to the end of the 1930s has been summarised in the weighty volume *British Textile Design in the Victoria and Albert Museum*, Vol.III, Victorian to Modern, by Linda Parry and Valerie Mendes, Tokyo, Gakka Co., 1980, with English and Japanese texts.) As at the Whitworth, the collection of post-war industrially-produced domestic textiles has been built up systematically by purchases and gifts from the progressive manufacturers, Heal's, Hull Traders, Liberty's and so on, and it can claim to be extremely comprehensive. The policy of acquisitions has been followed through right to the present day, with Designers' Guild co-ordinated textiles and the weaving and embroidery of the current crafts revival, work by Archie Brennan, John Hinchcliffe, Verina Warren, Kaffe Fassett. The most recent acquisition is a rug from Roger Oates.

Industrial Design is a bit more problematic. At the time of writing, it appears to be in a curious state of limbo. The Museum has a few key pieces of industrial design of the pioneering pre-war period, and some of these are on show (spasmodically) in the 20th Century Study Collections. But the main collection of British industrial design from the late 1950s onwards, an immensely interesting and potentially valuable hoard of past Design Centre Awards, is at present still in store, in a kind of basement no man's land, apparently unclaimed by any V & A department. One hopes that with the reorganisation entailed in opening the 20th Century Primary Gallery this unique design collection will resurface.

Meanwhile, the Prints and Drawings Department, as part of its normal policy of acquisition, has been building up an ever-growing collection of twentieth-century designers' working drawings.

Victoria and Albert Museum:
The Boilerhouse
Public/Study collection of industrial design funded and administered by the Conran Foundation

'The idea for the project arose' (as Terence Conran, its progenitor and chief financier, and Stephen Bayley, its Director, announced in 1980 in *The Designer*) 'because there didn't seem to be anywhere in the world where designers and those people who are interested in industrial design in its true sense could study a collection of products, and their related documents and back-up material.' All too true. This very admirable Conran Foundation enterprise has grandiose and optimistic plans ahead for a whole self-contained purpose-built design complex, including a museum and exhibition area, conference accommodation, a library and archives for the serious study of the design process. For the moment, the project is quite cosily ensconced at the Victoria and Albert Museum, in what used to be a genuine boilerhouse, beneath the buildings along Exhibition Road. As well as organising an exhilarating programme of public exhibitions on industrial design, the Boilerhouse sees its role as that of a collection centre for key pieces in the international history of design for mass production: intending to amass the ultimate collection of design for consumer goods, high style for the mass market. Because of its emphasis not just on finished products but on the whole process of designing, the Boilerhouse acquisitions policy is covering an immense amount of detailed back-up information: sketches, drawings, models (even models unaccepted); information on promotion and advertising; sales graphs. The whole gamut. Perhaps this brings a danger, which could well be self-defeating, of documentation obliterating product; as far as working drawings go, there is a boredom threshold which curators should be wary of. But these are early days.

William Morris Gallery,
Water House, Lloyd Park,
Forest Road, Walthamstow,
London E17
*Public/Study collection**

Water House was the home of William Morris as a boy, and the William Morris Gallery is certainly the best place to start looking at Morris's life and work. As well as some endearing memorabilia – the steel helmet Morris used as model costume armour for the Oxford Union murals, the chair that Morris actually sat upon while weaving – the Gallery contains a large coherent display of Morris's designs for textiles and for wallpapers, arranged informatively with biographical material on Morris and his circle, together with Morris & Co. furniture and carpets, and a multitude of drawings and decorative design work. An extensive and deeply interesting collection, only a fraction of which can be shown at any one time. The William Morris Gallery also houses major British collections both of the work of that very enigmatic Arts and Crafts designer A.H.Mackmurdo – with some rare examples of Century Guild furniture and fabrics – and of Mackmurdo's life-long friend, Frank Brangwyn. Alongside the many paintings and prints by Brangwyn, there are two very impressive pieces of his furniture (one illustrated on page 109), and a whole dinner service in the 'Harvest' pattern he designed for Doulton in 1930 (see page 97).

Besides the well-established public collections it is often worth investigating the (by their nature) more changeable displays of modern design in London galleries and auction rooms. A growing number have begun to specialise in the design of the past hundred years. For the Aesthetic Movement and Arts and Crafts, there are almost always interesting pieces to be seen at the Fine Art Society, New Bond Street; Haslam and Whiteway, Phillips and Harris and Richard Dennis, all in Kensington Church Street (Richard Dennis is an expert in Arts and Crafts ceramics).

For the period between the two World Wars, there are now several specialist galleries which have sprung up around Motcomb Street, in the shadow of Sotheby's, Belgravia; the Chenil Galleries along King's Road is also a good hunting-place for 1920s/1930s pieces. Jeremy Cooper, Galen Place, WC1, covers design 1830 to 1940. Post-war design is, in dealer's terms, still a fairly unknown quantity, though Sotheby's, Belgravia has recently tried hard with it. Design in current production is most easily investigated at (obviously) the Design Centre in the Haymarket, and the design-orientated stores: Heal's, Liberty's and Conran.

The Crafts Council Gallery in Waterloo Place; the British Crafts Centre in Earlham Street; the Craftsmen Potters' Shop in Marshall Street; and Liberty's One-off Department are the best places to start at for contemporary crafts. See also the directory of craft galleries in *Crafts*.

Manchester

City Art Gallery,
Mosley Street, Manchester M2
Public/Study collection

The main City Art Gallery, with its very famous collection of High Victorian and Pre-Raphaelite painting, has eagerly begun to buy the objects of this period. The Gallery now shows signs of becoming a total experience in Victorian design. Its many acquisitions of the past three years, Continental and British – including a superb Liberty 'Cymric' clock, a terrific Benson kettle – have been chosen with considerable flair. The collection of Late Victorian and Edwardian art pottery, especially the Royal Lancastrian by Pilkington's, with its strong Mancunian connections, has always been impressive and appreciated; the studio pottery of later periods – Cardew and Pleydell-Bouverie from the 1930s, Waistel Cooper and Geoffrey Whiting purchased from the Red Rose Guild in the 1950s, some good Rutherston collection 1970s additions – can be seen from time to time amongst the modern paintings in the Athenaeum galleries. Also, unknown to many, Manchester possesses a remarkable Industrial Art Collection of pottery and glass produced in the 1930s, amassed devotedly and with great discrimination, year by year, from 1929 until the War. Sadly, this, the most coherent collection of its period in the country, including fine examples of Keith Murray, Susie Cooper, Truda Carter, Harold Stabler, Eric Ravilious and many others, is so far, hardly ever put on show.

Whitworth Art Gallery,
University of Manchester,
Whitworth Park, Manchester M15
*Public/Study collection**

This is, on the whole, an admirable collection, in some ways a unique one, most intelligently organised. It covers the Arts and Crafts period with distinction, with some stupendous Morris tapestries and hangings, and a very good selection of Voysey, Day and Crane and lesser luminaries such as Lindsay Butterfield. There is something of a lull in the 1920s and 1930s: Ethel Mairet and Barron and Larcher are included, but machine-produced fabrics are poorly represented. The collection

219

springs to life again in the post-war period, with a massive holding of modern printed textiles, gathered in, year by year, from the contemporary ranges of Heal Fabrics, Hull Traders, Edinburgh Weavers, Warner's, Cepea and so on; a collection of enormous future value to historians. The acquisitions seem to stop in the mid-1970s, but one hopes that this is just a minor aberration: a collection built up with such expertise and diligence must surely be continued and expanded.

Norwich

Sainsbury Centre for the Visual Arts,
University of East Anglia, Norwich,
Norfolk
Study collection, occasionally on exhibition

The Sainsbury Centre, avant-garde symbol of the 1970s, has an extremely interesting small collection of an avant-garde symbol of the 1930s: the Isokon furniture produced by Jack Pritchard to the designs of Marcel Breuer and Walter Gropius during their brief working life in England. Part of this collection was presented by Jack Pritchard; some has been purchased by the University of East Anglia. The collection includes (how could it not do?) an original Isokon Long Chair with laminated frame in birchwood (see page 105). Now slightly battered, this is terribly evocative. The modern versions, although relatively faithful reproductions, somehow never look the same.

Poole

Poole Pottery Ltd,
Poole, Dorset
Study collection only

The potteries at Poole were at their most creative in the period between the two World Wars. In 1921, the designers Harold Stabler and John Adams joined Charles Carter and his son Cyril, owners of Poole potteries, to form a new subsidiary, Carter Stabler Adams. The designs which they produced, under the name Poole Pottery, quickly won approval in the DIA circles, and sold well at Heal's and Liberty's. Most of the shapes were the work of John Adams, most of the patterns were supplied by Truda Carter (first the wife of Adams, then the wife of Cyril Carter: the personal relationships at Poole were rather tortuous). In the public collections, Poole Pottery of this important period is quite well represented, especially at the V & A which in 1978 held an exhibition showing Poole right through the century; the exhibition catalogue is a particularly useful one. The pottery itself has now begun a collection, with a few superb examples of Truda Carter Primitive, as well as interesting pieces from the 1930s, by which time Poole was becoming much more stylish and commercial.

Portsmouth

City of Portsmouth Museums and
Art Gallery,
Museum Road, Old Portsmouth,
Hampshire
Public collection

The Portsmouth collection aims to show the development of British taste from the seventeenth century to today. No mean ambition; and, inevitably, so far, the collection is much stronger in some respects than others. But the acquisitions policy is conscientious, and where gaps are most apparent – as, for instance, in the studio pottery of the early twentieth century – the Museum is endeavouring to fill them. It also has a serious commitment to the buying of contemporary crafts. As it stands at present, the collection is at its best in its ceramics: a very generous coverage of the late nineteenth/early twentieth centuries (De Morgan, Martin Brothers, Ruskin,

Doulton, Della Robbia) and a substantial collection of modern craft pottery (not just the fairly usual Fritsch, Rie, Poncelet and so on, but more esoteric choices like Pepper, Lord and Mellon). The collection includes some interesting modern textiles (a rug by John Hinchcliffe on loan from Southern Arts, a specially-commissioned Margaret Smitten hanging depicting the Museum in its gardens), and the furniture on show illustrates with great effectiveness the U-turn in taste from the work of Ernest Gimson, represented by a staid and beautiful inlaid dining suite, to that of Nigel Shelley, a new craftsman, whose bright-red glass-topped table, which must seem very startling to some of the more solid of the citizens of Portsmouth, was added recently, with a fifty per cent purchase grant from the V & A.

Rothbury

Cragside, Rothbury, Northumberland
National Trust House

Between 1870 and 1884, Norman Shaw built this house; or, rather, he expanded an existing weekend villa to make a stately home fit for Lord Armstrong, the great armaments tycoon. In such a grand and eclectic kind of building, self-assured yet volatile, brilliant Norman Shaw baronial, there are bound to be echoes, and many premonitions, of national traditions. Cragside, of course, is full of them: in its intrepid, and successful, combination of the Anglo-Japanese with the Old English; its overtones of High Aestheticism; its hints of coming Arts and Crafts. There is even a vast fireplace, a ten-ton marble chimney-piece exquisitely carved in florid Renaissance manner, designed by – of all people – W.R.Lethaby, Shaw's chief assistant at the time of Cragside. Strange to reflect that 35 years later Lethaby was the great prophet of 'efficiency style', founder-father of the DIA.

Sheffield

City Museums,
Weston Park, Sheffield
Public/Study collection

The main expertise in Sheffield is in Old Sheffield Plate, of which the Museum has a renowned collection. The bias of this collection is, of course, traditionalist, and seen in this context, some good pieces of Dresser, who designed for several Sheffield firms, seem all the more remarkable for their innovation. Sheffield also owns some impressive Omar Ramsden – including the great covered cup we show on page 92 – and a small collection of Sheffield modern cutlery, some from the 1930s, some from the post-war period, which could, one feels, be usefully expanded.

Silsden

Morton Sundour Museum Collection,
C.H.Fletcher (Silsden),
Airedale Shed, Silsden, Keighley,
West Yorkshire
*Study collection only**

The Morton textiles firm has been the most consistently progressive in Britain in this century, through from its Arts and Crafts period – a fruitful one, with a whole succession of designs by C.F.A.Voysey – to the immensely influential Edinburgh Weavers' abstract collections of the 1930s and the large-scale printed textiles of the Festival of Britain period. The Morton Sundour archive, one of the very richest and most comprehensive modern design collections in the country, was maintained at Morton Sundour's headquarters in Carlisle (in large oak storage cupboards purpose-built by Gordon Russell) until, in the reorganisation following the takeover of the firm by Courtauld's, it was rehoused in the factory of

C.H.Fletcher, a Courtauld's subsidiary in Silsden. Here, perhaps indefinitely, it still is. Although the collection is in no immediate danger – it is kept in quite good order, there is no problem of access – this does, perhaps, raise fairly crucial questions about the right locations for important design collections. One sees the point about decentralisation: no one wants all major collections to be kept in London. But is there any sense, and any future, in siting a collection in a location with which it has no particular connection? The effect of this, in fact, in time could well be deadening. And, for practical purposes, for the convenience of the researchers and design students who would benefit from fairly frequent visits to the collection, isn't Silsden, in West Yorkshire, rather off the beaten track?

Southampton

Southampton Art Gallery,
Civic Centre, Southampton,
Hampshire
Public collection

Southampton has a marvellous, though not enormous, collection of the work of British studio potters of the 1920s/1930s, assembled in its period by the Very Rev. Eric Milner-White, late Dean of York, and given to Southampton, home of his father. (The other, larger half of the Milner-White collection was presented to York Art Gallery, *q.v.*). Southampton has a very good representation of Sam Haile, Bernard Leach, Charles Vyse, and especially Staite Murray, with some pots of extreme size and of great quality. More recently, to complement the Milner-White collection, the Gallery has bought some contemporary pottery.

With modern pottery at Southampton, Hove and Portsmouth, the South Coast is now a prime place for ceramicists' excursions.

Stoke-on-Trent

City Museum and Art Gallery,
Broad Street, Hanley,
Stoke-on-Trent
Public/Study collection*

The pottery collection in the new museum complex in Stoke-on-Trent is, understandably, a huge one, very catholic in feeling, not at all a purists' collection, but containing some remarkable material in each period. It has, to begin with, an exceptional selection of late nineteenth/early twentieth-century art pottery: some exquisite Pilkington, Bernard Moore and Ruskin, a definitive group of work by Edmund Elton, and many more examples, acquired early on in the Museum's history. It has the largest collection anywhere of pots by Michael Cardew, some superb ones, and work by other potters in the 1920s/1930s, in all around 500 pieces, bequeathed in 1949 by Dr Henry Bergen, friend of Bernard Leach. The Museum has also been active in buying modern craft pottery, mainly figurative, and has recently been concentrating on acquiring good examples of industrial production from the 1930s onwards, to balance its fine representation of crafts. Stoke-on-Trent is not afraid of the ephemeral and fashionable, and some mid-1950s 'Midwinter' designs by Terence Conran and Hugh Casson certainly have considerable nostalgia value. Among current acquisitions has been a useful collection of Susie Cooper pottery, both her pre-war and her post-war production, filling a small gap in British middlebrow design.

The Wedgwood Museum, Barlaston, Stoke-on-Trent *Public collection*	The Wedgwood Museum collection is historic, but in recent years it has been dawning on the Barlaston curators that the twentieth-century is part of history too, and the Museum now has some good examples of the work of Keith Murray and Eric Ravilious for Wedgwood in the 1930s, and the Coronation Mug designed by Richard Guyatt, in the idiom of Ravilious, fanciful and very British, in 1951 (p. 135).

Sudbury

Sudbury Hall, Sudbury, Derbyshire *Public collection*	This collection of modern ceramics, only started in 1978, is located in the somewhat unlikely setting of Sudbury Hall, one of the richest and most lavish seventeenth-century houses in the country. It takes quite a lot to compete with Grinling Gibbons; but the ceramics collection is, at first sight, a convincing one, with pots by Coper, Rie, Ray Finch and Michael Casson, Gwyn Hanssen and Val Barry, and others, knowledgeably chosen. A collection to watch.

Swindon

Museum and Art Gallery, Swindon, Wiltshire *Public collection*	In 1974, Swindon began a collection of modern British pottery from individual workshops. Before the gentle reader exclaims 'goodness, not another', let me explain quickly that the collection was started for the perfectly good reason that the area around Swindon has a long tradition of pottery; the relationship between the Gallery and the Department of Ceramics is a close one, and potentially profitable; the collection itself, with pots by Richard Batterham, Alan Caiger-Smith, Hans Coper, Lucie Rie, Katharine Pleydell-Bouverie and others of such stature, shows all the signs of being a sound one. And yet, though Swindon, it appears, has every reason for embarking on its collection of ceramics, and pottery of course is eminently collectable (being relatively cheap, quite easily available, convenient to store and fairly simple to display), it is possible to wonder, when faced with just so many collections of ceramics up and down the country, whether modern potters are being too much boosted, perhaps at the expense of other British crafts.

Totnes

Dartington Hall, near Totnes, Devon *Hall owned by Dartington Hall Trust, open to the public*	Between 1930 and 1938, the weaver Elizabeth Peacock was at work on her largest and most complex commission, indeed one of the most ambitious individual craft commissions of this century. This was the weaving of ten large heraldic-abstract banners for the great fourteenth-century hall at Dartington. The banners had a functional purpose, to improve the acoustics of the Hall, to make it suitable for the many musical activities of the Dartington Foundation. The banners also had a grand symbolic aim, to glorify the purpose of the Dartington community by representing the work of the various departments of the estate. Miss Peacock took the commission very seriously. She came from her home in Sussex to visit Dartington. 'She came several times', as Dorothy Elmhirst, co-founder of Dartington, recounted later: 'She spent long quiet hours sitting alone in the Great Hall absorbing the qualities and atmosphere of the building and soon afterwards began working on the first banner.' It is very moving to see those finished banners in the Hall at Dartington, in which they still hang now.

Wolverhampton

Wightwick Manor,
Wolverhampton, West Midlands
National Trust House*

Wightwick is a house very much worth seeing as the best example of a Morris and Co. interior which is still extant. The house used to belong to the Mander family – Theodore Mander, a local magnate, began building it in 1887 – and the present Lady Mander, a devotee of Morris and his circle, lives at Wightwick, as National Trust tenant, surrounded with what is still a quite extraordinarily vivid collection of Pre-Raphaelite paintings, Morris textiles, Morris wallpapers, embroideries and tapestries mingled, in the manner of the period, with antiques and Oriental *objets d'art*.

York

Art Gallery,
Exhibition Square, York
Public collection

At York the main claim to fame is the collection of ceramics given to the City by the late Dean of York, the Very Rev. Eric Milner-White, between 1951 and 1963 (the remainder of the collection is at Southampton, *q.v.*). It is a large and also a fastidious collection, totalling about 150 pieces, dating from the 1920s/1930s, when Milner-White first began buying pots from Bernard Leach, Staite Murray, Michael Cardew, together with some very good examples of Hamada; and extending to the Dean's later purchases, examples of the work of Leach and Cardew in the 1950s. York also keeps a small group of pots by William De Morgan, and, unusual in this area, the Anglo-Japanese not being much seen north of Watford, an E.W.Godwin ebonised occasional table and a second table Godwin obviously inspired.

224

Index of designers

Roman figures refer to book pages, italic figures to illustration numbers

General index